The Woman in 31

Decoding the Secrets of the Proverbs 31 Woman

A Journey of Faith and Empowerment

BRENDA HERON

WINNERS
PRESS

ISBN: 979-8-9925922-0-7

To my husband who taught me what it means to be truly loved.

To my son for your life-giving words: Breathe.

To my mother who never stops giving.

*To every woman facing barriers of time and "No"—God says
"Yes."*

Contents

Introduction: Woman's Journeys

It was a perfect June day. The city was alive with the vibrant energy of summer, and the warmth of the sun tempted us from the coolness of the café out into its golden glow. As I sat relishing the last few morsels of a tasty lunch, I glanced out the window just in time to see the red flash of a double-decker bus weaving through the street.

"Brenda, can I ask you something?"

I turned my attention back to my lunch partner, who was moving the tines of her fork around on the plate somewhat nervously. She was a beautiful young woman in her twenties, full of the promise of many bright years ahead.

"Of course, you can," I said, putting my fork down and folding my hands on my lap.

I studied the perfectly chiselled outline of her face as her dark brown eyes drew me into the heart of her concern. She was an eloquent, articulate young woman, but on this occasion, she lingered on each thought before she spoke.

"There's a major decision I need to make, and I need your advice."

As the conversation continued, she poured out her dilemma whilst I gathered my thoughts and drew on all the wisdom my years had afforded me. We shared experiences, and those I described reflected the many ways in which Father God had worked in my life. Her relaxed smile confirmed she had received the answers she needed.

"Wow, I feel so relieved!" She was practically beaming. "You should write a book, Brenda. I mean, *really!*"

Why I Wrote This Book

As early as I can remember, I have always diarised aspects of my life, but when the idea came to write in detail, the desire always slipped through my busy life. I finally realised that I had received something special, a unique understanding of an icon in scripture, the Proverbs 31 Woman.

The Proverbs 31 Woman has become a well-known title, her story passing down through the centuries to meet us today. Her life has been read countless times in formal settings and events of many kinds. She has been dissected over dinner tables and discussed in large and small groups, with no area of her life left unexplored. She has been researched, intellectualised, and blogged about, with countless books written to present the introduction, middle, and conclusion of the text about her life.

Her character has been carved as an immortalised model of perfection for all women everywhere. Yet we still question her reality and debate her attainability. When we reflect her mirror on our lives, we battle with various interpretations in an attempt to figure out how we measure up in her perfect world.

We read her story, ponder the narrative for a few hours, even days, and then she is quickly forgotten until her home in Proverbs 31 comes round again.

For years I read about this woman and then listened to the interpretation of her story from the perspective of others. I even attempted to speak about her to other women in conferences and small groups. Still, she remained elusive, unfathomable, and no comparison to my life. In all honesty, she was the woman I felt I could never become. So, I closed the chapter on her perfect world and moved on to make sense of mine, and our paths diverged. I shut the door on number 31 until she resurfaced to become the theme of a tribute I organised for my mother.

The Woman in Proverbs 31 provided the theme and content. My mother devoted her life not only to her family but also spent many years working alongside her husband to build our local church. She was a formidable, creative, and stoic woman who I felt in some way could be compared to the woman in Proverbs 31—although I had yet to fully uncover the depths of this figure through the Hebrew alphabet. This understanding would come later, following a life-changing event that I will talk about later in the book.

Look back to a time in your life that altered the course of your thinking and plans. It may have been a child leaving home, a painful end to a relationship, or the death of a close friend or family member. It does not even have to be an emotionally wrenching time; it could have been a relocation, career change, or reaching a certain age—so many possibilities. These times are what I term "transitions," which have a profound effect on your thinking and the course of your life. Transition well with the right support, and you'll discover a strength inside of you greater than you could have ever imagined.

When I discovered the Hebrew alphabet and its meaning, I realised it was the connecting bridge between the Woman and me. I was able to make sense of the transitions, and as you travel with me, you will too.

Wisdom Hidden in an Alphabet

In the land of ancient wisdom, where words hold the power to reveal hidden truths and illuminate the path to understanding, lies a treasure waiting to be discovered. This treasure transcends time and space, weaving itself through the tapestry of biblical texts, revealing secrets yet to be discovered. This treasure is none other than the Hebrew alphabet.

For centuries, scholars and theologians have grappled with the challenge of fully comprehending the Woman in 31. Who is she, this woman of noble character? What makes her so extraordinary? And how can we, in our modern world, begin to grasp the depth and significance of her identity and how it relates to our lives?

But what if I told you that the key to solving this mystery lies not only in the verses themselves but also within the very letters that form the words? What if I revealed to you that the Hebrew alphabet holds within it a profound understanding of the Woman in 31, offering insights that have eluded us for far too long?

As we journey through the ancient corridors of the Hebrew alphabet, revealing hidden secrets that have been whispered for centuries, together, we will uncover the hidden messages woven within the verses, shedding new light on the awe-inspiring identity of the Woman in 31. And with each turn of the page, you will gain a deeper understanding of her timeless relevance to our lives today.

A road on my faith journey, which I share in the course of this book, led my husband and me to study the Hebrew alphabet, or *Aleph-Beyt* ("alef-bet," as pronounced in Hebrew). It was an insightful time that furthered my understanding of the scriptures I had read for years. This time, the words I had read many times before left their almost ethereal plane to become concrete and, as I often describe, three-dimensional. What's more, my relationship with God my Father through His Son Jesus, Hebrew name *Yeshua*, deepened incredibly. Once you understand the secrets I'm about to share from my discoveries in the Hebrew alphabet, your relationship with Jesus (Yeshua) will deepen, too.

Share My Journey and See Yours

You will see that this book is multi-layered. First it is autobiographical in nature as I describe experiences in my life and examine ways in which my life events were and are linked to the description of the Woman in 31 through my understanding of the Hebrew letters. I also talk about Father God and the beauty of his work in my life as He has moulded me into the woman and wife I have become today, and this journey is ongoing.

During the early stages of this book, you will read about my first marriage in some detail. But, in all of this, it's important to know I have forgiven my first husband "seventy times seven," so there is no toxic energy. To do this I had to be willing to follow Yeshua's teachings on forgiveness, forgive myself, and allow

Father to heal my emotions and, over time, let go of the pain and the past.

Prepare yourself for a life-changing experience as you journey through our story—the Woman in 31 and my own—so that you can allow Father to open your story in whatever way He will work in your life. You will gain a newfound sense of self-worth and purpose and a deep understanding of your own significance. As you join me on this transformative voyage of discovery, I invite you to open your heart and mind to the unfolding wisdom hidden in the Hebrew letters. The secrets of the Woman in 31 await, and they are eager to be revealed.

"And I am certain that God, who began the good work within you, will continue his work until it is finally finished...."

—Philippians 1:6

Chapter 1

A Journey to Discovering Identity

ALEPH
Who can find a virtuous woman?
For her price is far above rubies.

It was one of those humid, thundering London summer nights where the heat of the day was disappearing slowly. It was the kind of night where you might have fans blowing on maximum speed with windows open wide as you watched the increasing flashes of forked lightning brighten and race across the sky. The visual theatrics of the night sky did not disappoint. The distant peals of rolling thunder would add further excitement until it arrived and boomed in the night sky to complete the summer's sensory feast. It was the kind of night where, space permitting, you might sit out in an open area or near a window, in fact, anywhere that offered a cool, dry space to escape the muggy city air longing for rain. When nights like this in London occur, you know summer has arrived.

I found myself in a repeating pattern of running and walking along the long, dark side road leading to my home. I was filled with anguish and remorse, and clashing thoughts moved around my head with kinetic energy. My life was an emotional mess; I had made an idiot of myself again, and I felt weak and foolish.

It started to rain, small warm spots at first, until heavy drops pelted down mercilessly. I had no umbrella, but I didn't care. I welcomed the heavy rain amidst the seeming hopelessness of my life. I gradually stopped running and instead walked and cried while experiencing the perfect mixture of rain and tears running along the contours of my face.

Lost in thought, I heard a vehicle's engine drive up from behind and slow down. Glancing to the right, I saw a small white van slow down until it rolled alongside me, but I was too upset to care. The driver rolled down the window.

"Are you okay?"

Without turning my head, I shot him a curt reply, "Yep." I clearly was not.

"You sure you're okay?" he asked, seemingly concerned.

"Yes, I'm okay, thank you," I repeated, then watched him slowly drive away, gazing at me through his rearview mirror.

Amidst the deep pain I felt, I was conscious enough to recognise that, on a late rain-filled night, someone stopped to care, for me, for a brief moment, but how did my life get to this?

Working Life

I was nineteen when I started working in the accounts office of the Magistrates' Court in Marylebone in London's West End. Exiting the underground on my first Monday morning, I was welcomed by the Victorian architecture of the grand and regal station. The court was located on the busy high street where prestigious buildings housed the head offices of many of the large retail companies. Well-established, tall trees lined the traffic-filled, four-lane main road. In contrast, the quiet side roads with their wealthy residences, fashionable businesses, and small independent retail shops offered a welcome relief from the noise and dense traffic fumes.

Tina was one of the few older women working as a court usher at the London Magistrates' Court, where I started my working life. She was a shrewd, older Barbadian woman who, like many, had come to the UK to build a new life. She had advised her daughter well in the area of real estate and was keen to take young, inexperienced women under her wing to offer business advice and "life skill growing up lessons," as she put it.

She would breeze between the teak-panelled courtrooms and the office dressed in the official flowing black usher's gown, holding under her arm the paper court lists of those who were to appear before the magistrates that day. Yet despite the formality of the role, she always wore a seemingly mischievous grin.

Tina often replaced the pauses and full stops in her conversation with sexual comments, which she delivered in an attempt to shock the young, seemingly impressionable women working around her, but her words escaped our attention, and I don't think she even realised. Despite her unsavoury innuendoes, from time to time, she offered good advice. "Buy property and rent it out!" she would say, repeating herself like a passionate schoolteacher, as if she somehow held a lens into my future.

The trouble was that, although I listened, I didn't act on the advice, and her words would float into my head for a brief mental process and glide out. I didn't ask enough questions or even understand which questions to ask, as my parents' financial advice had always been, "Save your money." Still, Tina invested time in explaining that her daughter was active in the property market, where she had made purchases for the purpose of renting. There will always be people we meet and opportunities that present themselves, and when they arrive, we need to be sharp enough not to miss those times. Years later I realised this advice was not only a missed opportunity at an early stage in my life but an uncanny foresight into the journey my life would take through numerous addresses.

The days of my first employment unveiled in me a conscientious young woman who worked well but lacked the confidence to take on more responsibility, so she never pushed to climb the career ladder. It's not that I wasn't ambitious, but fear stemmed from doubt in my abilities, so insecurity kept me comfortable in the mundane routine rewarded by a steady wage while those in senior positions and close colleagues persistently encouraged me to get ahead. I remember spending at least six months at evening college studying to be a paralegal, but without the confidence to move to the next stage, the course ended before that career path began.

The summer of 1988 effectively saw the end of my brief four-year career in the Magistrates' Courts as I flipped over to taste the fast, fevered, competitive world of recruitment. The new environment housed a constant, excitable, high-fever pitch of phone conversations as consultants chased clients for roles and matched candidates to vacancies. It was in extreme contrast to the role I held previously, where the mature and young mixed in steady-paced offices. This role was different. It was demanding and target-driven, where the fiercely competitive were pushed to succeed and increase company profits. My insecurities surfaced, and reasoning the post way beyond my ability, it only took three weeks for me to hand in my resignation. I later discovered I had hit all my targets, achieved the highest sales target that month, and had been given a bonus, but lack of confidence kept me confined to a small space. The following summer months met me unemployed and wondering where to go next. Without a clear idea of what I wanted to achieve going forward, I spent the remaining time organising the last days of my single life.

Confidence

I returned from my first holiday abroad alone, confident, and ready to push my life forward. This positive experience in Barbados with my cousins and an extraordinary aunt was a major turning point in my life. The trip had started on a dull and wet London day at the beginning of summer, and eight hours later, I arrived in the tropical country to be greeted by an elegant, beautiful black woman with shoulder-length hair and her face camouflaged by black, wide-brimmed designer sunglasses. My parents had spoken a lot about this woman, as the youngest daughter in a family of fourteen—with my father the youngest son—the siblings grew up very close.

Angela, as she was called, had grown up in the West Indies surrounded by wealth. She was known for her trademark expensive dark glasses, which shielded her rarely seen gentle dark brown eyes and complemented her love of fast, open-top cars imported from abroad. As my parents had often commented that I looked very much like my aunt's younger self, I decided to play her younger match and chose to wear dark sunglasses to meet my father's favourite sister.

When I arrived at Grantley Adams International airport, my Aunt Angela, then in her late forties, greeted me with a warm hug before stepping back to get a clearer picture of her young admirer.

"You do look like me when I was young!" Then referring immediately to my glasses, she proffered a brief razor-sharp lesson on designer eyewear. "Great look, but never, ever wear cheap sunglasses!"

I wasn't hurt but amazed and in awe of my beautiful aunt. I couldn't help but feel grateful for being offered wise advice from the woman my parents often talked about when recalling stories from their young days growing up in the West Indies. In my brief time away, I was keen to learn as much as I could from this woman I held as a role model. Amidst the many things we spoke about, the advice she gave that I never forgot was, "When you marry, marry for love." It seemed odd advice to give a young woman, and I wondered if there was more to tell beyond those dark rims.

My outlook on life expanded during my brief time away from the UK. My cousin, a few years younger, introduced me to the clubs, bars, and restaurants on the island, and we would drive home in the early hours of the tropical mornings to the sound of crickets and the distinct smells of the fresh, warm Caribbean air. We were careful to remove our shoes while walking across the veranda to not wake up my aunt and uncle. During my time there, I experimented with hairstyles and clothes, was introduced to a wide circle of people at house parties and later spent time with my cousins' friends who met up to socialise at different homes. In the evenings, we took trips sitting at the back of friends' trucks racing down long, dark, winding country roads while looking up to the Caribbean night sky filled with a million stars twinkling like diamonds and singing along at the top of our voices to the song "Everybody Wants to Rule the World." During those moments, I never wanted to go back to the UK.

Six weeks later, a changed young woman who had grown somewhat in confidence left Barbados. At that age, short experiences can make significant impressions that change the course of your life. And this was one of many. It was an evening flight from Barbados on a British Airways jet direct to London. I remember the plane taxiing down the runway and taking off above the hundreds of night lights, roads, and houses that turned at an angle, slid away, and reduced in size. As the plane rose higher, I whispered *Goodbye, Barbados.* I felt sad to leave. Despite the promises to return, I somehow felt that I would never see my aunt and cousins again, and this was certainly true of my aunt. Twenty-four years later I would meet my cousin again—at my father's funeral.

A Meeting

It was with this new confidence that I met my first husband five months later at a house party in East London, which turned out to be a birthday celebration. It was a surreal moment, played somewhat in slow motion, as I looked over towards the entrance of the room to be attracted by a man with a wide smile and perfect teeth! I remember asking his sister (whose birthday it was), "Who's that guy?" and hearing her distinctly high, excitable voice as she shouted his name and immediately introduced us.

For some reason, I had spent a lot of time thinking about what to wear. At the back of Oxford Street in London's West End where I worked, stood a myriad of small wholesale shops selling clothes and accessories to the fashion industry. Some sold directly to the public, and, over the many times I had passed the shops on my way to and from work, I sometimes stopped to buy clothes and got to know a few of the owners. I wore a beaded, ivory dress that evening, which fit my young body like a glove and with no stomach to pull in. As I followed his exuberant sister across the room to join the new path in my life, I felt dazed, and everyone in the room faded into the distance.

Our first time together was spent in a small cinema on a summer evening in London's theatre district watching *The Colour Purple*, where the world was introduced to the acting talents of Oprah Winfrey. My stomach was crammed with nervous excitement as somehow I knew this meeting would be my first serious date. I had earlier turned down an invitation to accompany him to a charity gala in London's Mayfair as I wasn't prepared to be overwhelmed by both the event and being with a man I sensed was special.

The following day, flowers arrived at my home with a small card. I was impressed. My father opened the door to the postman and called me to collect my package. The family had been invited to an August wedding, and we were just about to leave when the flowers arrived arranged in a clear plastic oblong box. I read the card discretely placed on the side as my father watched without trying to be obvious. I couldn't have scripted happier moments during the following months, leading to an engagement; everything seemed perfect.

Living at home I shared a room and memorable times with my two sisters, and, being the eldest, I was the first, in some ways but not all, to push the boundaries until it was time to leave home and start a new life. As we drove along the tree-lined streets into the middle-class suburb with its large homes, open green spaces, wide pavements, and streets arrayed with mature trees, my first impression of South London, the new location where I would live after we were married, was daunting; a sharp contrast to East London. Meeting my future husband brought new social circles where I would either engage in or just listen to the conversations of aspiring, ambitious young people, where dreams and plans were obtainable.

Compared to me, my first husband always seemed more relaxed and comfortable with his identity, career, and achievements. On the other hand, I was young and impressionable, and future events that were about to play out signposted the journey to carving my purpose and value.

Reflecting on that period, I see now that I was in a season of transitions, each change shaping my path in ways I couldn't fully comprehend. I sought new directions through a career change and evening studies. The timely advice of a court usher provided guidance just when I felt uncertain about my next steps. Then, meeting the man who would become my husband added another layer to my journey. Was the Woman in 31 the key to understanding my evolving identity?

~

Woman or Wife?

Before we explore the first Hebrew letter, *Aleph*, linked to the first verse, I want to explain my choice of using "Woman" rather than "wife." During my research, I found several translation choices for this Hebrew word. The traditional King James Version (KJV) translates the Hebrew word as "virtuous woman." Other translations—such as The Aramaic Bible in Plain English and the JPS Tanakh (Hebrew Bible translated from the Masoretic Text)—use the word *Ishah* as "woman." Versions such as the New International Version (NIV) and the English Standard Version (ESV) translate the word as "wife." I discovered, however, that "woman" and "wife" are the same. I will explain.

In Genesis 2:23, when God presented the woman to Adam (Hebrew: *Ish*) he named her "woman" (Hebrew: *Ishah*) as she was taken out of his side, and then later, Adam calls her "woman person" (as described in the CJB), his "wife." The Hebrew meaning of Ishah means, "woman," "wife," or even "bride," but the basic meaning is "female." Later in Genesis 3, Adam calls his wife *Havah*, meaning "life," since in her new role, she becomes "the mother of all living" (Genesis 3:20 CJB).

Throughout this book, I use the term "Woman" as an umbrella under which we, as women, function as wives and mothers or as effective singles. Whatever course of life we are on, God has fully equipped us to be fruitful in every area as "Woman."

Unravelling Her Character

Proverbs 31, in the Bible, is found in the last chapter of a series of wise sayings. It is described as a Hebrew *acrostic poem* where each verse is linked to the twenty-two letters of the

Hebrew alphabet. The writer of most of the proverbs is known as one of the wisest and wealthiest men in history and one of the many kings of ancient Israel; he was called Solomon. You may have heard the famous saying, "To everything there is a season, a right time for every intention under heaven—a time to be born and time to die...a time to tear down and a time to build."[1] Solomon wrote those sayings. The woman in the poem is described in Hebrew as *Eishet Chayil*, which translates as "a woman of valour."

For Her Price Is Far Beyond That of Rubies or Pearls

Some translations have chosen rubies instead of pearls as the precious commodity to which the woman is compared. Keep in mind that the writer is stating that the Woman's value is greater, but as a starting point, let's consider the pearl.

Pearls are formed inside an oyster as a defensive mechanism against parasites, yet these irritants become catalysts for the pearl's change and transformation. When the hard, outer, beautiful oyster shell is pried open, the precious pearl appears. This pearl represents every woman whose trials and challenges shape them into something precious and beautiful. God is developing her character to meet the challenges of what I describe as "irritants"—transitions, commitments, and responsibilities in the home, family, workplace, and business—and yet, despite the challenges, if she chooses, she is able to live from God's Life which supports the statement "For I can do everything through Christ, who gives me strength."[2]

1. Ecclesiastes 3:1 Complete Jewish Bible (CJB)
2. Philippians 4:13 New Living Translation (NLT)

I firmly believe that a woman, whether working alongside her husband or leading a single life, is a powerful agent of change in both public and private spheres. From the very beginning, God equipped her with every skill and ability to fulfil her purpose: "I knew you before I formed you in your mother's womb."[3] The daughters of Zelophehad in the Bible exemplify this truth. Brave, knowledgeable, and determined, they fought to change the Mosaic law, securing the right for women to inherit land in the absence of a male heir and ensuring their family's legacy was preserved.

The description "Christ who gives me strength" applies to absolutely every situation, challenge or irritant we face, which are common yet different for every woman. Christ supports us through the changes, demands, twists and turns, and as we emerge from fragility to strength, we realise the irritant had a purpose, and a pearl is produced.

The Meaning of Aleph

Aleph, pronounced "alef," is the first of the twenty-two letters in the Hebrew alphabet. In ancient Hebrew, letters represented as drawings were known as pictographs. The letter Aleph was represented as an ox head, as shown here:

---

3. Jeremiah 1:5, Galatians 1:15

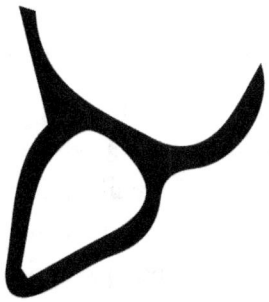

In this acrostic poem, Aleph is the first letter in the Complete Jewish Bible (CJB) attached to the tenth verse, "Who can find a virtuous [good] woman? For her price is far above rubies" (KJV). Interestingly, the Hebrew letters of the alphabet have numbers and meanings. The meaning of Aleph is "strength," "powerful," "leader," and "beginning." The Hebrew spelling of the word for "Father," *Abba*, is made up of the two Hebrew letters Aleph and *Beyt*. Aleph means "strength" or "leader," and Beyt, the second letter of the alphabet, means "house" or "tent."

Taking a closer look at the two Hebrew letters spelling the word for "Father," we discover the full meaning as "the strong, powerful leader of the house." God presents himself as the strength of our lives. In the New Testament, Jesus presents a story to illustrate the spiritual message of a man who built his house on a rock. Houses represent lives, and the woman's emerging purpose and value, the core of who she is, comes from building her structure on God, The Rock, who she learns to trust as a true Father.

~

Unravelling God's Work in My Life

From very early on, although I didn't always recognise the way God worked, He continued to introduce Himself to me as the "strong, powerful leader" of my life. My aunt, who I described earlier, the people He sent, and the many experiences He put my way were to develop confidence and continue building my identity. In certain ways, Tina, the court assistant, brought valuable experience in buying and renting property. What I now realise is that when useful information comes our way, although it may seem way above and beyond what we understand at the time, we should pursue it. I needed to research the property business and ask more questions. It could be said that this is retrospective thinking and only valuable long past the opportunity, but Father wanted me to act on that advice.

This understanding became valuable much later as I began to understand the way God worked in my life. As the Strong, Powerful Leader, God wants us to know He constantly thinks about our lives and has plans for us. Knowing about God and how He works in your life is the difference between merely hearing about Him and truly experiencing His presence. It's like buying a new car and feeling all the excitement—talking about it, cleaning it, sitting in the seat, and looking at it—but never actually driving it. But when we finally decide to drive the car, knowledge and experience meet. The often-used but sometimes unclear phrase "relationship with God" becomes meaningful as we begin to understand His ways and how He works in our lives.

The move to the recruitment agency was tough and a complete contrast to the slower pace of the Magistrates' Court, but this was the irritant God was using to help me grow in confidence and understand my skills. From the moment I started work in that busy open-plan office, I met a woman at the coffee machine, and we had a conversation. That is when God began to identify Himself to me as the "Leader."

She was around my age, and having been a consultant for a few years, she offered to support me during the first few months. With her advice, I hit my sales targets earlier than most, but not realising that Father was leading me through this job, I left feeling that I couldn't cope in such a pressurised environment. It would take a few more years for me to realise that Father, silently yet loudly, had been at the forefront of my future. The Strong, Powerful Leader was guiding me through the everyday events to build my identity in Him, developing confidence so I could see my abilities.

Purpose and Value

By showing the Woman's purpose and value, the Proverb begins by describing "her price" as "far above pearls." There is so much to say on that, but it is beyond the scope and purpose of this book. Many of us have struggled and maybe still continue to struggle with accepting our value and worth. Multiple factors such as family background, relationships, socioeconomic circumstances, body image, the ever-changing societal norms of beauty, sexuality, and gender roles become prevalent factors and variables in recognising and establishing value and purpose. Our struggle is further enhanced by an environment unrelenting in presenting its opinion of exactly who the woman should be and the skewed societal values she should use to form her identity. I believe, however, that characteristics are developed and moulded over a lifetime of experiences linked to the challenges and change God presents.

"Oh, that you would choose life, so that you and your descendants might live!"[4]

In 2017, the "Me Too" movement, started by Tarana Burke in 2006, gathered pace on social media and went viral. It originated from one woman's determination to end shame, years of silence, and intimidation in the face of a brick wall of sexual harassment, abuse, and rape culture. The movement, initially igniting a trickle of women, soon became thousands who stood together in solidarity against sexual harassment in the workplace. As women realised their worth, they opened the door for others from all ethnicities, classes, and cultures to join hands, identify with one another, and speak out.

Women, and later men, from all cultures and industries identified with this movement, and the response was powerful. There is strength in numbers, but true strength comes from women recognising their purpose and value. Doing so gives the deep satisfaction of finding the roots of who you are, what shapes you, and where you fit within your environment, all of which have the capacity to affect the present and future.

Father gives identity, value, and purpose. He supports His Words with actions that prove a woman's worth is priceless beyond pearls. From the beginning of all time, the Woman was given her role, purpose, and value to function at maximum in her life. These are His Words:

"Then God said, 'Let us make humankind in our own image, in the likeness of ourselves; and let them rule over the fish in the sea, the birds in the air, the animals, and over all the earth, and over

---

4. Deuteronomy 30:19 New Living Translation (NLT)

**every crawling creature that crawls on the earth
....' God blessed them: God said to them, 'Be
fruitful, multiply, fill the earth and subdue it
....'"**

—Genesis 1:26–27 CJB

This supports the statement I made earlier that Father valued
the woman, His creation, and gave her everything she would
need to function at the highest level and in her role alongside
her husband to be productive and increase.

God doesn't change and has not changed His mind. When God
stepped into a human body, Jesus, and walked the earth, He
met with many women, from mothers to single women, married
women, young and mature, business women, women who
worked as prostitutes, women in ministry, and rich and poor
women alike. He met women from all walks of life who were
kept hidden by laws and traditions. Now, because of Him, we
are not hidden; we are free to live and be productive in all areas
of our lives as the Women He created us to be.

Identity and a Strengthening Sense of Self

Many have said we model ourselves after significant people in
our lives or those we admire. The type of childhood we
experienced growing up and the female role models in our lives
—mothers, caregivers, family, friends, teachers, and other
figures—have played an important role in shaping our identity,
purpose and value. However, as our lives move forward, our
present becomes the past, and hurtful past episodes hold a
power with the potential to become silent tormentors. This
blocks our ability to see the capability of the woman facing us

in the mirror and the potential of the woman waiting in the future.

God reveals an aspect of His character to us as "Mighty." We find this meaning in His name, *Elohim*, and the full revelation of who He is through His Son Jesus, Yeshua. Our identity becomes the first connection He wants us to make with Him as "Strength," the core building block and central to understanding who we are as women. This block is moulded over a lifetime of experiences. We are not weak, and I'll talk more about that later.

Trying to make sense of who we are stems from asking self-directed questions, "Who am I?" and "What am I here to do?" Although we're not asking these internal questions daily, experiences force us to look at ourselves in an attempt to make sense of our lives. This process of questioning and self-evaluating, in my opinion, happens over a continuum as we are constantly re-evaluating and re-shaping ourselves. If we are looking to Father, the Strong Leader of our lives, we will regularly take time to ask these questions when we speak to Him and look for His replies in our everyday setting. He will guide us in our purpose and roles as women, whether we are wives (working alongside our husbands) or single women where God is the Head.

Our strengthening sense of self is the beginning of the shaping of our identity in the strength, power, and leadership of God, who is the Aleph and number one in our lives. Before anything else in Proverbs is written about us as women, like the Woman in 31, God first wants to give us a true and strong identity on which we can build our lives.

The environment we face can be hostile and unrelenting in its subtle and sometimes forceful concepts of identity, so God defines the woman's identity by the attributes He possesses: power, strength and leadership. This is the first carving out of our value as women, led by the Aleph, the Head and Strong Leader of our lives. On those days or times in our lives when we feel completely depleted and everything other than what He wants for us, we can come to Him for encouragement. Through this relationship, God gives us everything we need to operate our lives a step at a time. His ability is inside us, but we can only see these qualities when we look in the mirror at the woman looking back at us and accept the affirmations He is giving.

"Virtuous" Is Not a Weakness

When we look at the Hebrew word for "virtuous," we find the word *chayil* which translates as "army," "strength," "wealth," "force," and "ability and efficiency." These descriptions tell us that identity is formed from a position of strength because these are God's never-changing character qualities, and He has placed these qualities inside us, allowing us to start strong, despite how we feel. Life experiences will search and find our weaknesses to build God's characteristics in us.

For years Proverbs 31 has been read to countless women, and we have all rehearsed and repeated its verses in our heads. But in reality, we have felt quite the opposite from this perfect painting of a woman. You may have wondered, *Who is she? Is she real? Does she even exist?* Is this ancient portrait of a woman carved centuries ago out of touch in our lives today? How can we make sense of her seemingly endless capabilities? What about everything else she seems to do so perfectly and effortlessly? She's like a woman with the perfect life.

Interestingly enough, some Jewish writings explain the poem was written for King Solomon's mother, Bathsheba, and if you read her story, you learn she had her own issues! She wasn't perfect at all! So what did Solomon see that inspired him to write for her? Perhaps she saw the woman who she had become over years of experience and the identity she had formed. Contrary to popular belief, the poem was far from depicting a perfect woman and wasn't written to place unrealistic expectations on future generations of women or to show a man's ideal.

In response to "Who can find a good woman?" —the opening line of the poem—the question we could ask then is, "How can I apply this woman's strength to my life on Monday morning?" or "Who will find me?" I say God has already found us and given us an identity carved from Himself and modelled by His Son Yeshua, Jesus Christ. This requires a mindset shift.

Chapter 2

Learning to Trust

BEYT
Her husband trusts her from his heart, and
she will prove a great asset to him.

I was the first to leave a close family of two brothers, two sisters, and loving, hard-working parents who had given up much for their children to give the best start in life, which for them was being formed in a new country with a new culture and customs. We were raised in a Christian home where the church was central to our lives. The people we met became extended family as we were all from similar cultural backgrounds, which meant certain prerequisites were already in place, leaving time to build on other aspects of the relationship.

Often on weekends, we were invited to different homes where several families would meet to enjoy seemingly never-ending plates of home-cooked foods and discussions to share experiences of life in the UK. The adults, or "the big people" as we called them, would talk for hours about matters we were too young, too busy, and had no interest to listen to.

Amongst our noisy, boisterous play in the rooms nearby, we would hear the rising sounds of loud discussion and laughter, then the fall of hushed tones suggesting private conversations as we entered the room for more handfuls of finger foods after a large meal. But, as I mentioned, those matters didn't concern us. I was a young girl, and it was my time to have fun with friends and siblings.

During my years growing up, observing and listening to my parents, I could honestly say that they lived the words they spoke with passion and consistency and raised us in a home that reflected the love from the scriptures they read to us. It was their silent modelling of faith in everyday life that became a functional reality later on. Up to the day my father passed, they were a couple in love with God through Jesus (Yeshua) and each other, with a vibrancy and ability to enrich the many lives of people around them and beyond for years to come.

Weekly, our family would spend an evening together praying and discussing family matters, school, and home. It was at those times when my parents would encourage and gently steer us in a direction towards knowing God for ourselves. Although the church we attended set strict boundaries, we were raised in an environment that allowed space to think. And when the time came to make life decisions, which we did, and in directions they would not have chosen for us, they gently let us go. We were, and are to this day, a very close family.

The Diamond and the Champagne Flute

I wasn't different from the other young women I knew. I wanted to be in love, get married, and have children, imitating the pattern I had seen from my parents. Shortly before my wedding, the realisation hit my mother that her eldest daughter was getting married and soon to leave home.

I had made my decision and accepted the proposal to get married, but my mother had reservations. It wasn't that she did not like the man I was choosing for a life partner, but she wondered if, at twenty-three, I was ready to get married and more so to a man she felt had much more life experience and several years between us. However, my mind was set; I was ready to leave home, but she felt uncomfortable with the process.

After a few meetings with my future husband, my parents spent many weeks praying and discussing the decision to let their eldest daughter go. They finally agreed to support the marriage. My mother took a little longer to feel settled, which I never really understood then, but much later on, as life experiences increased, I began to appreciate the reasons why perhaps she felt that way.

Weeks had passed, shrouded in a long, uncomfortable silence that eavesdropped on my parents' private conversations. In the back bedroom I shared with my sisters, this silence grew louder each time I pondered my father's decision. One evening, as I sat alone in the room while my sisters were elsewhere in the house, I heard the familiar sound of my mother's footsteps echoing down the hallway. The three steps that separated our room from our parents' added a rhythmic elevation to her quick, decisive pace as if her feet were racing to be the first to share some urgent news.

The door opened, and my mother came in, sitting gently on the edge of the bed.

"What do you know about this man?" she asked softly.

"I love him," was my only answer, and that, I guess, was enough.

We got engaged at a restaurant in London's famous Covent Garden on a summer evening at the height of Prime Minister Margaret Thatcher's '80s. It was a time when people were spending and living to financial excess; purses and wallets were crammed with multiple credit cards, and people craved ever more fiat currency. I remember my future husband proposing and presenting the diamond ring we had designed. The scene remains framed in my memory, similar to those idealised romantic comedies where all the diners come to a stop, applaud, and whistle.

That was my scene, and I said "Yes!" the moment he presented the ring. The diamond sparkled as I paraded my left ring finger over a glass of Cuvée Rosé Laurent-Perrier. Then, just as he was about to fit the gold band, it slipped and fell into the champagne! The action played out in slow motion, and I laughed as I watched him fish it out from the bottom of the champagne flute. The hilarious moment passed, but was it indicative of the grief and pain that was to come for both of us? I won't cloud the memory because, at that moment, it was perfect. We were perfect, in love, and excited to move our lives forward together.

The Tollgate

In a small room on the first floor of an unassuming bridal material shop in Enfield, a suburban town on the outskirts of London, my mother, aunt, and I agreed on a small sample of beaded and sequined ivory wedding gown material. The order was placed for the fabric to be flown over from Paris, and my aunt, an experienced dressmaker, cut the dress to the detail of my pencil-sketched design. My cousin also helped with sewing the beaded initials of our first names onto the long, raw silk train.

On a warm May morning, my mother and aunt circled around me with the grace and precision of two professional dancing partners. I stood like a mannequin in my parents' bedroom, overlooking the quiet street filled with childhood memories of playing with neighbourhood children as the two sisters perfectly synchronised their moves to dress me for my wedding.

Memories floated back to Sunday mornings when the family prepared to attend our church, which was a few miles away. The bells from the local church at the end of our street would ring a melodious tune across the neighbourhood. Later, the marching band would step in rhythmic unison to the beating of the drums and the blowing of the brass instruments. With excitement, we'd run to the window and look down onto the street to see the band dressed in bright uniforms and heads lifted high, proud to welcome Sunday morning. Later, as a young adult, it became the street I would walk down in the early hours of the morning, shoes in my hand, so as not to wake my parents asleep in the main bedroom with its single glazed sash windows poised to let in the quietest sounds.

We were married in a small, picturesque 19th-century church located midway along a small village lane near one of London's last surviving tollgates. The vicar kindly agreed to conduct the wedding alongside my dad, who was also our pastor, and my new life began. My eldest brother, John, taking the role of my father for that part of the day, sat with me in the wedding car and played the perfect part.

On the long route from East to South East London, a hilarious moment relieved the nerves we both felt as, looking down at his shoes, John noticed he had forgotten his shoelaces! The wedding cars stopped for my brother, dressed in a grey tuxedo, to race into the local corner shop to save his shoes. Later, with great pride, he played his part and walked me down the long aisle to the music of Ravel's Bolero until I stood next to my future husband.

Pouring out from his heart a wellspring of carefully selected wise words forged from experiences, my dad spoke eloquently and with candour in front of family and guests.

"Won't they have hard times?" He posed rhetorically. "Won't they have difficulties? But God will see them through."

The thoughts he expressed seared into my memory as if they knew they were to become reality.

I remember looking up teary-eyed as he spoke; my heart flooded with mixed emotions of deep admiration, love, and happiness as my father loosened the hold on his eldest daughter. He passed on his experiences, explaining that he had proved God to be the foundation to navigate all of life's events, happy and sad. Then, after having the wedding blessed by Dad and the Vicar, an ecstatic twenty-three-year-young, married woman and her husband turned to face the world and a new life.

The reception passed with all the joy weddings bring, but the one moment that remained vividly etched in my memory was the feeling of change I experienced. As I stood and watched our guests dancing, eating, drinking, and having conversations, the music and guests seemed to fade into the background, leaving me to stand alone in the large Georgian hall. In that poignant moment, the reality of my new marital status washed over me like a powerful wave: I was no longer single and no longer looking for a relationship. I was married and now an outsider to that world, standing on the periphery looking in, observing where I used to be.

We left the reception accompanied by a cascade of rice and confetti lovingly showered upon us by family and friends. As we drove off in my new husband's car, I looked down at the grains and colourful specks that clung to the front and inside of my dress, seemingly marking the transformation within me.

Goodbye for Now

In all of the day's events and experiences, regrettably, I don't remember saying goodbye to the closest women in my life, my mother and two sisters. But years later, we would form the strongest bonds from the sum of experiences life was getting ready to throw.

The day had whisked me away, and I was eager to begin. But before I leave that moment in my life, there is one more memory of that day that stands out. At some point during the wedding day, my husband leaned over to excitedly whisper the news that our offer on a house we had viewed and fallen in love with a few weeks earlier had been accepted by the seller, and we were soon to exchange contracts. Along with all the unforgettable memories of a dream day, we could not have scripted a more perfect sequence of events.

The Meaning of Beyt

Beyt, the second letter of the Hebrew alphabet, is pronounced "bate," meaning "house," and the numeric value for Beyt is two, which signifies either division or a double witness. The letter is linked to the eleventh verse of Proverbs 31:

> **"Her husband can trust her, and she will greatly enrich his life."**
>
> **—Proverbs 31:11**

As we move through the twenty-two letters of the Hebrew alphabet, we will find they take us on a journey through life. Having looked at the first Hebrew letter, Aleph, in chapter one, we discovered it represents God, the "strong, powerful leader." Looking then at the meaning of the letter Aleph and linking it with Beyt, the second letter, we see that Aleph, the "strong and powerful leader," is the Head of our house or lives.

Father is the Head of our lives, and by "lives," I mean the way we think, our sense of self and all other areas which make us who we are as individuals. While we can connect and relate through shared experiences, each woman is unique in her own way. When we allow Him, Father becomes the Head and takes the lead in our relationships, family, friends, careers, and every other aspect of our lives. This doesn't at all mean we move through life passively, but we trust Father and involve Him in our processes with the recognition that His desire "above all things" is for us to "prosper and be in good health even as our soul (thoughts, emotions, decision-making) prospers" (cf. 3 John 1:2). Father is concerned about all aspects of our lives.

Trust unfolds as we stop, take a deep breath, and exhale while relying on Father God to head up our lives and bear the weight of our life experiences. How does that happen? We choose to relinquish control of our lives by believing that God's desire is to see us fulfil the destiny he has designed for us. God is invested in us, and His desire is to see us win. This brings rest to our everyday lives, allowing us to think clearly. We choose to speak His promises into our situation despite the challenges, and over time, our thinking and words change. As we come to accept that God operates in many different and interesting ways, we will begin to understand Him in a deeper way, just the way our human relationships develop. But the difference here is that God, the Aleph and Strong Leader of our lives, will not let us down.

Trust

God is establishing us and building the basis of who we are as women first by assuring us, like the Woman in 31, that He trusts us from the core of Himself—His Heart—because that's the area where we are positioned—in His Heart—irrespective of the opinions we hold about ourselves. He simply trusts us, so we shouldn't be afraid to trust Him or ourselves and move forward in life.

For some of us, due to relational issues we have faced, whether from our broken or abusive relationships in our childhood or as adults, trust is one of the biggest challenges we face. The ability to trust others and ourselves deeply impacts our confidence, sense of self, and well-being, and knowing we struggle with a lack of confidence in certain areas can be a lifelong challenge, with issues moving in and out of our lives like waves.

The response to these emotions is to learn to Trust God, the One who knows us explicitly. Men have trust issues too, but Father is firmly saying to women, through the Woman in 31, that He trusts us from the core of His Heart. He reaffirms us and raises our self-esteem by expressing the fact that He trusts us first.

That statement needs time to sink into our thinking as we get on with the business of life. On days when our confidence is lacking, we're inadvertently asking, "Do I trust myself?" Maybe the real questions are, "How does God feel about me?" and "How do I feel about myself?" God makes the statement, "He trusts her from his heart," which applies to us; He trusts us, and we will be a great asset to Him. This should give us confidence to trust ourselves, trust the decisions we make, and, over time, develop trust in our significant others.

Father views our lives as His "house," His "Beyt," a place where He can fully invest in us all that He has to give once we invite Him in. The scriptures tell us that we are His house, and He lives in us.[1] Not only are we God's House but we live in His house, which is His heart. In this statement, Father God shows us how He feels by saying, "I trust you," "You are My house," and "You are an asset to Me."

As women, over time and living out our everyday experiences, accepting this position in God's Heart should be enough to give us the confidence to achieve anything in life without mental

---

1. 1 Corinthians 3:16 TLB

barriers of where we live, cultural backgrounds, or social and economic status. We are at the core of His heart, and from that strong position we have the ability to push forward with our lives.

If we understand that we hold an important position in God's heart, then taking time to listen, we will hear His heart. We hear Him through the words we read, in what He says to us, and in the many different ways He speaks to us through our everyday lives, even when we know nothing of Him, having only heard of a God who lives in places of worship on the weekend or represented in pictures or carved images that can't see, hear, or feel us.

~

Decisions

On the first meeting with my first husband, on that August summer day, I believe God's answer was "wait," but I was determined to push ahead with my decision and plans. The weekly family meetings where my parents taught us the scriptures, the discussions that took place, praying together, and watching my parents' lives were the early days of God showing me His ability to be the Strong Leader of my future home. My parents took many weeks to agree to the marriage and give their blessing. I now know it was because they wanted me to wait and take time to think through the decision I was making. My mother's words suggesting I should wait was Father showing Himself as the Strong Leader of my life—if I had listened and allowed Him to lead—but I understood that the decision was mine and mine to make, and He wasn't about to override it.

A few weeks before the wedding, my fiancé and I argued. At some point, it was as though I stood in the room alone for what seemed like a few seconds, and as I looked at the man I loved and was about to marry, I felt quite strongly that the answer to my early prayer about marriage was "wait." I argued with my thoughts briefly and reasoned things would settle after the wedding.

On that amazing, happy wedding day in May, without realising it, I was now asking God to establish the house—the Beyt— between myself and my husband in a marriage covenant. However, I didn't fully appreciate that, right there, on that day, it wasn't just about getting married to the man I loved, but, like the meaning of Beyt, we were standing as a "double witness" to the life-long marriage covenant. We were asking God, the Aleph, to be the Leader of the lives we were soon to begin behind door number 2A.

Chapter 3

Developing Resilience

GIMEL
**She works to bring him good, not harm
all the days of her life.**

Intrusions

The late eighties flaunted a time of excessive lifestyles and an overinflated property market. During this time, I transitioned from my childhood home to a new life in a wealthy south London suburb. Over many discussions and plans, my husband and I talked about our dreams, followed by hours crammed into days working to build our future. My husband, dedicated and passionate, worked tirelessly. His focus filled much of the time in our young relationship, and although I shared a similar motivation, my efforts were no match for his intensity.

The sale of his apartment, where we spent a good part of the first year of our marriage, allowed us to buy a large three-bedroom house, and our plans began to take shape. We were glad to sell the apartment since the property was burgled within weeks of returning from our honeymoon. I remember taking a call from my husband at work as he gently broke the shocking news, leaving as soon as I could to make the journey home, which seemed to last forever. His home, which I had just begun to share during the first months of our marriage, had been intruded, our space violated, but there was more to come.

One morning during the late summer, we took some time to have a quick breakfast together. Minutes after leaving, my husband returned looking worried, explaining he couldn't remember where he'd parked the car. He went out for a second search, but when he returned, we realised the car had been stolen. The vehicle was a company car we'd been using as our main form of transport as we had previously sold our cars to raise money for the wedding. Summer solstice had not yet arrived, but that day seemed the longest and marked the start of what I describe as "intrusions" in our relationship, with many to follow.

Later that year, with property legalities now completed, we moved from the "honeymoon apartment" that had been my husband's first home. Parents and a few close friends arrived early afternoon to help us carry boxes into a small, hired van to drive the short distance to the house where we would soon be living. As the property handover had been agreed for mid-afternoon, we spent the remaining time lounging on the soft ivory carpet in the now empty, large front room of the home where we had started our marriage. I remember the sun pouring through the Victorian sash windows and being overcome with a distinctly strange feeling, a warning, maybe. It almost felt as if the flat was trying to warn us of gruelling times ahead.

Door 131

Waiting in the van a few yards from our new home, we were excited at the prospect of moving into the house and starting the next chapter in our lives. The woman who sold the house was a professional cook and ran a business nearby. From what I remember, she baked and delivered to local businesses from the large kitchen in the house, which we later renamed "the cook's kitchen." From brief conversations, we discovered she had spent many years living in the house with her husband and raising a family, but sadly the marriage ended in divorce.

On the day we exchanged contracts, we met at the property, where she handed over the keys that opened a door for us and closed one for her. To this day, I still remember the moment she turned to look back at the house for the last time as she walked away. Her eyes were filled with tears, and her head with thoughts that I can only now guess. It was a brief moment, and then she quickly walked towards her car.

The faded pale blue house stood alongside a row of terraced houses on an incline leading up to a well-known outer London conservation area. Similar to the flat we had just left, the large property captured the sun at the front of the building through its large sash windows, which, even in the winter, made the front-facing rooms continually warm and bright.

The main room on the ground floor, with its double-fronted bay windows, had two fireplaces, and later, we discovered that the small wooden garden shed was filled with logs. As soon as the days grew colder, shorter, and darker, we couldn't wait to rush home to light both fireplaces, park ourselves on the floor to get warm, and listen to the crackling sound of the dry logs burning while watching the flames dance around in their contained space.

One of the amusing memories was that despite the many places we could sit comfortably in the main room, we found a tiny space, more like an enclosure, behind a single-seater leather chair positioned in front of the main bay window. We preferred the small space to have drinks and eat our meals; it was our special place, hidden out of sight in that large house, away from the world. It seemed especially carved out as a safe place for a young, married couple to hide away from the trouble ahead.

The focal feature of the large kitchen was a black, cast-iron Swedish wood burner with a large funnel rising into the roof. In the winter we burned paper and kitchen waste as it was a cost-effective and enjoyable way to quickly warm up the kitchen when we didn't want to turn on the central heating. I loved the house and was never reluctant to share aspects of our lives with the neighbours during conversations.

The house next door had been converted into two flats, which was fast becoming a trend at that time when landlords devised plans to make as much money as possible in the over-inflated housing market. I was excited and proud of where we were in our lives and innocently explained to our neighbours that we had bought the entire property, not realising how boastful that may have sounded. But I was young and confident, although naive about outside perceptions of a passionate, young couple with big plans for the future.

Details of the day I'm about to describe played out in sharp focus because it was the time, I believe, that started the downward slope in our lives. We had not long moved into the house and were still settling in. That bright Saturday morning, I stood in the kitchen cutting and arranging flowers in a glass vase. A friend we had recently met was giving away kittens, and after some discussion, we agreed to have a cat. Not having grown up with animals, I was unaware of my cat allergy, but the idea was appealing, and I loved the thought of having a pet at home. We left during the day and returned in the early evening with this tiny kitten nestled in a box on my lap.

As we drove up the short incline to the house, my husband remarked that the lights were on. We had left during the day, so there would have been no reason for lights. We got out and walked towards the house, and as we came to the front door, we noticed it was slightly open and a large kitchen knife lay on the floor in the hallway near the main door. My husband suggested I wait outside while he went into the house to check it was safe. We realised later that although the lights were switched on and the kitchen knife was on the floor, everything else in the house lay undisturbed except for one room we used as an office. A few days later while searching through items in the room we used as an office, my husband discovered important documents were missing, including bank cards. The early intrusion signalled the beginning of a financial spiral.

A few days after the burglary, my husband went to the cashpoint and was shocked to discover a large withdrawal of £500 that neither of us had made. At that time, there were no limits on maximum daily cash withdrawals, so over a period of a few days, several £500 withdrawals were made from different cashpoints in the local area. These withdrawals were from the money raised from selling my husband's property. With the car went the money, and the bank refused to compensate us, stating we had breached security by leaving the PINs with the bank cards. Although this was not the case, we were held liable for the financial losses. We were devastated and alarmed at just how quickly our situation had turned.

Months later, on a dull cold day in London, we were driving along a road not too far from where we lived. Feeling low because of the bank's decision, I thought I recognised what looked like a few of my personal items strewn across the road not far from where we lived. We stopped the car, and I got out. As I walked closer, there they lay like litter on the road. This now felt like a violent intrusion, a crude exposure, and a harsh introduction to a new life.

Work

I was determined to make a success of our new business and young marriage. Everything in my life felt unfamiliar and off course—it was. Moving away from family, living with my husband, moving to a new neighbourhood and having to familiarise myself with a different part of London and its culture, managing a home and a business, and getting to know myself all formed part of this new road in my life.

Towards the end of the first year of our marriage, my husband fulfilled his dream of starting a business and proudly opened the first delicatessen not far from where we lived. He called it Benjamin's after my birth surname, with the slogan, "Fine Foods, Fine Wine." We were now business owners and, to an extent, in charge of the direction of our futures.

On the first day the shop opened, he proudly wore a shirt and a bow tie, similar to the uniform he wore when he managed a well-known delicatessen off London's Knightsbridge. Although, at the time, the business seemed somewhat out of touch with the area, people unfamiliar with delis and the type of food sold began to take interest. The bagel soon became a popular alternative to the sandwich, and some customers with their South London accent would order a "bye-gul," which always made us laugh. However, much of the food we sold was new to me, too! We stocked a wide selection of fresh and dry foods such as cheeses, mustards, pâtés, cakes, quality olive oils, and vinegars. It was a steep curve, but I learned quickly, and after a few months the business began to attract the local artisan and media community, and trade began to increase.

The shop became the focal point in the area, particularly since a bus stop with multiple South London routes was located immediately outside, which meant we attracted more passing trade as people waited and looked through the windows. We soon became familiar with our regular customers and their lives, and they returned the interest to us, particularly my husband, with his elegant communication style and inspiring personality.

Often, we could sense when people wandered in to buy a coffee their underlying reason of wanting to chat. We learned a lot from our diverse community, and they probed us with endless questions aimed at discovering how we managed to set up our business. I think people were curious and wanted to know more about this young entrepreneurial couple, developing a new, unfamiliar business serving fine foods and wine in a less desirable part of London. We later found out we were the unwanted topic of conversation amongst neighbours who were eager to find out the source of our ability to buy such a large property. I was a twenty-four-year-old young woman on yet another steep learning curve to understanding people and intentions.

One afternoon, a conversation developed with one of our regular customers. The shop was quiet, so there was time to talk. Her comments hung over me for many years until Father helped me understand the harm behind the words and the healing in my life that later followed. She was around four feet nine inches tall, with short, black curly hair and large, deep brown eyes. I don't know why I remember this detail, but she only ever bought single items.

Unlike our many regular customers, it was difficult to predict this woman's buying habits. The transaction was always punctuated with the usual conversational pleasantries and small talk, after which she would return the following week. Then, after a year of the same generic conversation, just as the exchange of words came to an end, she explained that she had always wanted to own a business; then she commented on how "lucky" we were as she shifted her attention between us, the shelves of dry goods and the deli counter. During her visits, she would often repeat the same remark until one morning when she casually but confidently explained a dream she had seen where she saw our shelves empty. I don't remember ever seeing her again, but a short time later, her "dream" appeared to have become a reality.

In the most challenging of environments, during the three years we had the business, my experiential and life skill learning curve was exponential as I learned to craft words and conversations in social situations. One embarrassing but funny moment I remember was a remark I made to a woman who worked as a theatre stage manager. As I watched her walk into the shop, noticing the slight curve of her stomach, I excitedly decided to pass a loud congratulatory comment. She immediately shot back that she wasn't pregnant but had gained weight! I closed my large mouth, utterly embarrassed, and I don't remember whether we ever saw her again. My steep learning curve was a mixture of joy and crushing moments, conversations and silence, laughter and tears, energy and lethargy, and a lot of maturing, which I had to do—quickly.

She Works to Bring Him Good Not Harm All the Days of Her Life

Benjamin's quickly became our manager. It set the hours, days, and nights we would work if we were going to make it a success. The yearly rent for the building was exceptionally high, and despite the fact the property had been empty for years, the landlord determined the rent was non-negotiable. We discovered he managed many freehold properties across the UK. As the profits from the business slowly turned to losses as the recession grew deeper, my husband would literally set aside every penny of the shop's sales accumulated over the weeks to make the long drive to North London with the payment to meet the rent deadline.

Our Friday evenings, when we used to relax together, quickly disappeared in preparation for the busy Saturday trade. I had no previous experience in food retail and little knowledge of the effort it would demand. It challenged me in every area, from the early mornings setting up the fresh food counters, the long days serving customers, through to evenings storing and packing away the fresh foods into the large storage fridges at the back of the shop for the next day. On Saturday evenings we would completely clear away and wash down the counters to the sound of loud music at the end of a long day. Still, the tough work schedule was made easier due to my husband's experience in time-efficient ways to clean and prepare the business for the next trading day. Shattered, we would drive home to eat a late meal.

The early morning visits to the wholesale meat market brought another new experience. We alternated the duty between us, using our small, round white van nicknamed "The Bubble" to carry the goods. The 4:30 a.m. wakeup was always gruelling, with a half-hour window to dress and be out at 5:00 a.m. armed with the list of stock items for the shop.

I became a familiar face amongst the early-morning traders. I adjusted my eyes to the movement of people and my ears to the numerous friendly sounds of truck horns used to warn and move people traffic aside. This was the bustle of London's Billingsgate Market with its army of forklift trucks full of crates and boxes driving in all directions to offload goods to the nearby stalls and men running around in white overalls identifiable only by their business logos. However, my determination and focus braved the sounds of the loud male voices, raucous laughter, and the crude humour of the market sellers coupled with semi-naked calendar girls hanging on the walls of the tight-spaced, box-like booths where the assistant took cash-only payments.

Despite the organised busyness of the morning and the male-dominated environment, the men were always helpful and kind, and somehow, despite the fact that I was often exhausted by the morning market rush, the thought of an early breakfast just as the sun was rising was always welcoming. I don't remember praying much then, in a way that involves going on your knees, but I know I spoke to God a lot. The business—though new and demanding—was character-building, a life-shaping experience with a string of bitter-sweet memories. However, our marriage, at the centre of the plans we made, was about to experience pain beyond what could ever have been imagined.

$\sim$

Abba is the Aramaic term for "father" and is linguistically derived from the Hebrew word *AV* pronounced "arv," meaning "father." Interestingly yet purposely, the two Hebrew letters Aleph and Beyt—which spell the word "father"—also carry meaning as individual letters: "the strong leader" (Aleph) "of the house" (Beyt). God is known by many names and titles that give us a glimpse of the many aspects of His character. It compares to the many names we have for family and close friends that we use at different times, depending on where we are and how we feel. In our families, relationships, and amongst close friends, we may choose to refer to them using special names that we would not use in public. When we call God "Abba," this indicates that we are His children.

I mentioned door 2A at the beginning of this for a reason. After getting married, this was the number and letter of the door to my first home. The Hebrew meaning for both the number and letter was significant, which I will now explain.

I realised Abba Father walked through door number 2A in ways I only now understand. In the previous chapter, I explained the numeric value for Beyt is two, signifying "a double witness" or "division;" Beyt also means "house." The letter "A" is the first letter of the English alphabet, and the first letter of the Hebrew alphabet is "Aleph," meaning "strong and powerful leader." All along, even though I had rushed ahead of His timing, Father had already gone ahead of my life as the "Strong and Powerful Leader" and was again to stand as a "double witness" to all I was about to experience as I stepped through door 2A.

I'm not suggesting we should be looking for meanings in letters or numbers to understand our lives. Rather, we learn to rely on God, through His Holy Spirit, to help us see clearly and make the correct links. However, there are many biblical verses that do attribute meaning to numbers. Above everything, we just need to learn to trust God and accept that an answer won't be found for every question.

The Meaning of Gimel

The letter *Gimel* is the third letter of the Hebrew alphabet. It has a number value of three and is linked to the twelfth verse in Proverbs 31. The early pictograph form of the letter was shaped like the foot of someone walking, representing progress or movement; symbolically, it was also viewed as a camel. In ancient Middle Eastern culture and today in some countries, camels are viewed as symbols of wealth and endurance as they can sustain long trips in the desert. The letter Gimel is linked to God's eternal, enduring kindness to us.

The meaning of the letter represents Father who entered our world through His Son Yeshua (Jesus) to lift us up and unite us to Himself. In the books of the New Testament, Yeshua said, "I AM the way—and the truth, and the life; no one comes to the Father except through Me" (John 14:6 CJB). We have to walk to the Father by the Way, Jesus, who lifts us up.

The beginning of my journey to understand how God works in my life started with hearing about God, but it didn't stop there. The journey continued the day I said, "I do," but the next stage was the walk to get to know Him. My sense of pride about marriage, home, and business wasn't misplaced, but when they became consuming areas in my life, I developed an increasing reliance on what we, as a couple, could achieve through our abilities rather than the need for developing trust any further.

God's heart is for us to progress in our interests, skills, or passions, but the success we are looking for comes from Him as He develops our characters and gives us the confidence to achieve. The burglaries and slow erosion of our finances forced me to ask questions and search for answers from God, and over time, I slowly began to understand how God was working in my life, and the words I heard and read in the Bible became relevant.

Anna

I spent a large portion of my time in the shop, with early mornings and long days stretching into evenings. God reached out to me through customers I met who made me smile and laugh on the days when the pressure was intense. The country was still going through a deepening recession. Profits were sharply dwindling, forcing my husband back to paid employment to earn extra steady income, so we agreed I would run the shop alone during the day. The 8:00 a.m. to 7:00 p.m. days were long and exhausting, and by the time I left the premises, it was late into the evening.

The afternoon moved along its usual slow pace following the lunchtime rush, leaving me time to people-watch through the large floor-to-ceiling shop windows to the busy high street. As I prepared the counters for the late afternoon flurry of customers, a young woman strolled into the shop to buy a few deli items for a quick evening meal. I placed her purchases on the counter, and a conversation unfolded and extended for what seemed like hours as we talked and laughed. We connected and realised we had much in common.

Escaping a broken relationship, Anna was about to be made homeless with two small children. Although I couldn't identify with her situation, I listened and tried to understand as much as I could. Friendship and conversation were what we both needed—another woman to listen. We didn't share faith on the same level, but we could talk about life, and when the time came to talk about beliefs, Anna listened. My sisters and close friends lived a long distance away, and the pressures of time and the lives we were trying to build separated us for a while. Anna became like a sister and someone I could talk to.

Fern

I first met Fern through her young daughter, Julie, who breezed into the shop with her bright smile, curly long brown hair and precise pronunciation to confidently enquire about work. Julie explained that she had been watching the shop since it opened, and she and her mother had admired the young business owners. Julie was now keen to work with us. We had earlier discussed the need for staff, so the following Saturday, Julie started work. Each day she attended, she seemed to release a brightness into our lives with her fresh, positive outlook, commitment, hard work, and ambition to succeed in life. Then, when she spoke about her mother, I looked forward to meeting the woman.

Fern was a small lady at around five feet tall with a petite frame, but her high-pitched voice, intuitive character, sharp wit, ability to listen, and bubbly personality made her the tallest person in the room. Her long brown hair framing her pale porcelain features was always fixed perfectly, along with her smart sense of dress. Over time I learned Fern was a shrewd woman who seemed to understand ways to navigate life, and those who knew her warmed to her caring and generous nature. She became like the big sister I never had, and I welcomed her into my life.

Her home was filled with items she loved to collect from antique shops, boot sales, and her travels, and the aromas of her Trinidadian or "English with a Trinidadian twist" cooking was always welcoming. Time permitting, we spent days shopping, searching through curious items at boot sales or simply sitting, cooking, and chatting for hours about our lives. Fern was a woman who had stories of the many life journeys she had experienced, and her presence was invaluable to a young woman who was travelling far too quickly to stop and process.

Our lives eventually diverged, and then one morning years later, we literally bumped into each other in London's Dulwich Village. I remember the year because the United States had welcomed its first black President, Barack Obama. The timing was perfect. We hugged, pleased to see each other, and made a promise to meet, not understanding the reasons we had drifted. We kept to that promise, and time passed yet again, with us reuniting intermittently. Fern and Julie were among the many ways Father enriched my life, and I hope theirs.

Beginning to Fragment

I was working hard "to bring my husband good," building on a young marriage, home, and business. There was nothing wrong with that, but somewhere in between, I was beginning to fragment, and I didn't know how to fix things. At the time I couldn't see that God, as "the wealthy man," was working alongside, behind, and in front of me.

As women, we are constantly working in one way or another, whether in the workplace, at home, in education, or in commitments, all place a demand on our strength, character, time, home, and relationships. We may be working to build careers, we may have left the workforce to focus on family, or we may be balancing working or studying from home while managing children. A career now ended, whether due to redundancy or time for change, we may be working at a new phase to bring new experiences and financial support to our lives. We may be building on close relationships or playing supporting roles within extended family or friends. In all we are trying to achieve, we find ourselves trying to be strong for everyone while sometimes, without realising it, life slowly wraps us up until we become invisible to ourselves.

The description of the role of the Woman in 31 in this verse is symbolic of God our Father, the Aleph and Head of our lives, presenting Himself to us as the "wealthy man" who, through Jesus His Son, is able to meet us in every area, at every new phase, in every change, and at every decision. He is the "wealthy man" who bends down into our lives to give us what we need from His resources so we can get up and keep going.

This is not a linear progression of events but a cycle in which God is meeting us at every new phase to lift our lives and move us forward. His meetings with us occur on a daily basis, but we don't always realise it until we face major tests. At each stage we are given something valuable from the "wealthy man" to bring to the next experience.

We plan our lives, pray, and receive what we need—to work. We don't lack anything when we understand that Abba provides what we need to live life for the rest of our lives. This is how we are able to "work hard" or, better still, work smart throughout our lifetime. In an attempt to understand the Woman in 31, we can make the connection to our lives by analysing her character. We're not supposed to measure up to this description with its strong visual imagery of perfection. Instead, we admit our needs are His strengths and that God, the "wealthy man," will always meet us in ways we would not expect.

Chapter 4

Created to Create

DALET
**She procures a supply of wool and flax
and works with willing hands.**

Money

It was another warm summer morning, and the sun shone through the skylight as we sat at the breakfast table. It was time to talk about money. The breakfast table was where we did the calculations and reviewed the figures. We looked at the mortgage repayments, household income, and expenses, and things looked okay.

The year we were married, my husband made a profit from the sale of his property. Now two years later, seated at the wooden kitchen breakfast table on a sunny autumn morning, it was time to discuss money. The economy had crashed, interest rates soared from around eight to fifteen per cent, and our monthly mortgage repayments shot up by hundreds of pounds. It was a crazy time. We were yet to experience the crushing effects of having all our savings stolen with no investments to cushion the loss, and it wasn't possible to borrow from family and friends as the amount was too large.

The downward economy began to hammer our young business and regular customers, and passing potential customers had tight budgets with less to spend. We had less money to meet the household and business commitments, and until my husband went back to work to earn a consistent wage, we ran the business without staff as we could no longer afford to pay salaries. The punishing mental and physical routine of struggling to make ends meet was unrelenting. The shop was a public place, which meant there was nowhere to hide from creditors and debt collectors who would appear without warning armed with their Notice of Removal papers fixed onto the clipboards they carried with the intent of removing our possessions. The extreme pressure we faced began to affect our relationship. We were young, and maybe mutual expectations were high and often unrealistic. Besides our parents, we had no one to turn to for spiritual, business, or financial advice, so we inevitably turned our frustrations on each other.

Clinical psychologist Meg Jay defines the twenties as the "defining decade of adulthood"[1] when life and the brain are changing, and personality is being forged. Married at twenty-three, now moving nearer my thirties, I was changing quickly. I began to view life differently, and my changing experiences were shaping the opinions I once held. During the often twelve-to-sometimes-fourteen-hour days, there wasn't the mental time or space to make sense of those changes, and the

---

1. Meg Jay, *The Defining Decade: Why Your Twenties Matter—and How to Make the Most of Them Now* (Twelve, 2013).

time we needed to talk and resolve issues was consumed by work, late hours, and exhaustion.

One evening, in the heat of an argument while driving home in The Bubble, our small white van, I became overwhelmed with the problems we were facing and chose to run—run from the arguments, run from my life. I opened the door and managed to jump from the van just as we pulled up to the amber traffic lights about to turn red. It was dusk, and I clearly remember running down the long road and onto a busy motorway while the drivers sounded their horns, shouting at me to get out of the road. I don't know how I managed the next few moments, but I was able to climb up a grassy bank and over the gates into a children's playground, where I sat on the swings weeping as dusk faded into darkness. I don't remember how long I sat there; without a mobile, there was no way of calling anyone. As I sat there, lost in my messy, emotional world, I remember looking up to see the silhouette of my husband walking towards me. He sat, and finally, we talked. What we didn't know then was that this incident was just the beginning of many difficult times.

Despite everything, my faith in God remained a constant in my life. Although there were so many questions about the challenges I was facing, I was learning to trust Father on days that were shattering, despairing, or emotionally crushing. I didn't have all the answers for the reasons my life was following this route, but I knew Father wasn't going to drop me as I always remembered the words, "For I know the plans I have for you, says the Lord. They are plans for good and not for disaster, to give you a future and a hope." (Jeremiah 29:11).

∽

The Meaning of Dalet

The character reference in this verse is about the woman's readiness to work. Throughout the stages of our lives, Father gives the strength and ability to work across a wide and diverse spectrum of roles within our families, community, and the marketplace. The Hebrew word for "work" or "to work" is *asah*, which also means "to make, create, construct, build, and accomplish." There are many verbs, but I prefer to use "create" and "accomplish," as they reinforce the nature of our Father's work from the first day He began.

Before talking about the fourth letter of the Hebrew alphabet linked to the description of the woman in the thirteenth verse of Proverbs 31, I'll explain my interpretation. The short stay outside London and the house moves I have written about up till now saw the beginning of the many doors I would have to walk through during my life.

Despite the regular, sometimes mundane routines we face, no two days are exactly the same. So we should aim to take a different perspective and approach to the work we do and view it as "creating." While we appreciate the daily activities, although familiar, none of these activities are surprisingly new. Inevitably, there are days when we feel demotivated or despondent, when it seems things are not coming together as planned. These are the days when we feel alone, and people aren't around for support, or words spewed have been discouraging. The challenges life throws at our families, health, relationships, and employment can appear grinding and severe. But God, the Strong Leader in our lives, is generous and kind and will reach down to lift us up. He is the stability in our lives who gives new hope and trust on a daily basis, and our Father's consistent support helps us not just to work but to create.

Jesus showed us how to pray with the right words, "Give us the food we need today." (Matthew 6:11 CJB). He understood each day carried its own highs and lows, let alone having to worry about subsequent days. This new approach takes a gradually changing mindset, evolving over time, as we begin to realise that, like the Woman, we are always creating.

Staying Connected

The Hebrew number value for *Dalet* is four, and this number is connected to earth, stability, and creation. On the fourth day, God finished creating the earth for us (Genesis 1:14–19). Amazingly, the four Hebrew letters in God's name speak of stability. Also, the meaning of the Hebrew letter Dalet is "doorway" or "path." Jesus said, "I am the gate; If anyone enters through Me, he will be safe..." (John 10:9 CJB).[2] He is the Way we connect with God our Father. As we stay united to God, relying on the strength His Spirit gives our human spirits, emotions, and bodies, we can continue to "create." During those very tough years of my young adult life, God's Holy Spirit kept me connected from one day to the next without my realising it. However, I was about to see more of the strength of that connection as time moved on.

Despite All Efforts

A year later, despite all our efforts, we were heavily behind on our mortgage repayments, sharing the same predicament with thousands of people across a country in deep recession. We had

---

2. John 10:9 CJB

explored the few options available to keep up the payments, and one was renting the property and moving about sixty miles out of London to stay with my husband's parents. We rented our house to a young family on a short stay in London and moved in with his parents.

Our regular motorway commute worked well for the first couple of months until it began to drain us mentally and physically. We woke at 5:00 a.m. to drive the miles to London, where we opened the shop at 7:00 a.m. and prepared the deli counters for morning customers at 9:00 a.m. The usual day ended at 6:30 p.m., except when days were extended for stock purchases at cash-and-carry. We would return to the shop late evening to unload, then drive back along the dark motorway.

There were times our journey was filled with long, stress-induced arguments and, at the same time, our characters were evolving in this pressurised capsule where we tried desperately to make sense of our lives and each other. In the days leading up to our marriage, I remember my husband saying he would be there with me through the changes I would inevitably make. But although he was seven years older, in his very early 30s, we were still quite young, and when that time came, we didn't know how to be there for each other. So, we began to tear each other apart from the core. And when life challenged us to sink or float, we began to sink.

By the time we arrived at his parents, we were so worn out that there wasn't time to eat or talk. Some evenings I just wanted to greet my in-laws, pass on dinner, and go straight to bed. Trying to snatch a piece of normality after a long day, we would sometimes detour to visit friends before going back to his parents' home. We often arrived at the couple's house exhausted from the long day and motorway miles. Thankfully, they were welcoming and understanding.

It was winter then, and our friends' home was always warm and inviting, with low-lit lighting in the front room where they spent the evenings talking or watching TV. I don't know how they tolerated it, but there were times we would fall asleep on their sofa during conversation. True friends!

Marital challenges and tiredness characterised that short season in my life. Constantly exhausted, isolated from family and friends, without knowing how to handle the pressure, myself, my husband, or the business, I was becoming depressed and isolated. We were far from London; I felt detached, and the arguments increased. There were no mobiles, so the landline was the only way to contact friends and family. But in reality, relationships with my friends had become distant, and my sisters were trying to make sense of their own lives, so I wrapped myself in thoughts. God heard all of those thoughts just as the scriptures say:

> **"O Lord, hear me as I pray; pay attention to my groaning. Listen to my cry for help, my King and my God, for I pray to no one but you. Listen to my voice in the morning, Lord. Each morning I bring my requests to you and wait expectantly."**
>
> **—Psalms 5:1–3**

Letting Go

Try as we might, after a tough battle, we lost the beautiful and bright Victorian home with the large grey door, where we spent the first two years of our marriage. The rental income received from the property was stretched thin to cover our personal expenses, mortgage repayments and the young business. As we walked towards the court to end that part of our lives, I looked at the large, mature trees that lined the street filled with four-storey Georgian houses. The road, laid with Victorian pave stones, led up to the small white county court that stood waiting. Visually beautiful as the area was, it contrasted sharply with the feeling of impending loss of our home and the efforts we had made to save it. There was a feeling of emptiness as we walked along the quiet road to repossession and a partial end to our dreams.

The Large Grey Door

We slowly opened the large grey door of house number 131 to begin removing furniture and possessions, which were divided amongst our family's homes and space we had in the shop. It was distressing to have this happen, and it felt like our lives had been dissected and exposed. As we left the house, I stood at the top of the stairs outside the main bedroom, looking down the corridor towards the room opposite. There was a strange feeling of finality far beyond that of losing the home, and I sensed it would be a very long time before I would ever own a home again.

Door 181

Exhaustion, a demanding young business, and lack of money and time were variables contributing to the breakdown of a young marriage. In a desperate attempt to save what we were trying to build, we decided to move back to London and rent a room. I call this time in our lives "Door 181."

The house was located in an affluent area of South East London, bordered by several parks and one of London's famous heaths, Blackheath. Driving to the property, a twenty-minute journey from the shop, it felt like we had been thrown a lifeline to a fresh start, and that felt good. Suddenly there was more time in the day, and even though it meant we would now have the extra expense of rent payments, our petrol costs were reduced.

A few steps led up to the dark green front door of the semi-detached Victorian house at 181, which, after a few knocks, was opened by a woman who looked to be in her early fifties. She was tall with a slight frame, and her mid-shoulder-length light brown hair seemed not to have changed in style since the sixties. We followed her into the faded eighties-styled chintz front room, where we sat on the large sofa for a "getting to know you" conversation. I would intermittently glance around the room to take in the heavy yellow-stained walls while inhaling the lingering smell of cigarettes. However, Anne, our new landlady, was warm and welcoming, unmoved by our ethnicity. I liked her straightaway.

We spoke late into the evening. She explained that she was coming to the end of a divorce after forty years of marriage and was about to put the house on the market, so the rental would be a short six-month availability, which was all the time we needed. The evening ended with Anne showing us the fair-sized room with its two single beds and a small wooden table and chair. The room, located at the front of the house, overlooked the main road through its bay windows. In retrospect, the single beds at both ends of the room seemed to make early predictions of the route our marriage would take. But as a young, still newly married couple desperate to build our lives, it wasn't a problem. We were simply relieved to have found somewhere close to the shop and pleasant enough to live.

We left with the keys to Anne's front door and our new room, happy, excited, and relieved, and door 181 became the fourth house I had lived in since getting married three years earlier. Whatever and however we felt, we had been given a chance for a fresh start. During our time at 181, Anne and I had many chats where she encouraged me on the days when my husband and I had quarrelled as the marriage continued under stress. Even amid her troubled marriage, she spoke fondly of her many travels and identified the moment in South America when she sadly realised her long marriage was over. With tears in her eyes, she recounted the moment she was nearly hit by a bus, unnoticed by her husband, who had long walked ahead.

The first weeks in the room at 181 were happy times, and it felt like God had given us time to breathe and another opportunity to work on our relationship. My husband bought a quaint second-hand bike from an antique shop in East London. In the evenings, when we had a chance to leave the shop together, we would take the bike with its heavy metal frame to the heath, taking turns to ride.

Those summer evenings were always special because we spent time together outside of the business to talk, ride, and laugh. The bike later became a second form of transport as I would cycle the fifty-minute journey to the shop, returning at the end of the day to face the challenging cycle ride up the hill's steep gradient on a bike with no gears. Having reached the top, the journey was rewarded by the expanse of the large green heath that rolled out for miles on both sides of the road, and the air was fresh. It was always a welcoming and relaxing sight and a relief from the busyness of the shop and densely populated area. By the time I reached the top of the hill, my muscles ached, but the flat surface that followed allowed for an easy ride home to our room at the top of the house.

Sadly, the misunderstandings and arguments continued to escalate, as did the money issues. For a second time, we made the decision that one of us needed to earn a regular income, and this time, it seemed sensible for me to leave the business. Short but sweet, in every sense of the word, the break from the demands of the business was a welcome relief. I discovered hidden strengths and abilities. It was an amazing time, and I enjoyed the role I took as the manager of an ice cream parlour in London's famous Harrods. Although the tiny counter was tucked away in an area under the stairs in the grand Food Hall, it served a constant flow of customers.

I worked with an energetic, interesting team of young people around my age who were working to either support their studies or as routes to full-time jobs. At the end of a long shift, I would return to the room, which quickly became a lonely place as my husband spent long hours working. The room became a place for arguments, tears, and painful emotions, and despite how much we tried, we struggled to make our relationship work. I became miserable and depressed and constantly wondered how our problems had reemerged so quickly from those relaxed summer evenings on the heath. Then one day in autumn, after almost eighteen months, we decided to move into the flat at the top of the shop in an effort to save money and have our own space and front door. This next part of the journey took me through door 275, the fifth door.

The Day Before Christmas Eve

On the day before Christmas Eve, we moved into the apartment above the shop. The tall, three-storey Edwardian building needed significant repairs. We had already spent much of our income turning the empty shell of the ground floor into a business, which drained all the resources we had left. We accessed the apartment through a side door that opened to face narrow wooden stairs where we had to tread carefully to avoid putting our foot through broken, wooden steps. The rickety stairs wound round to the first floor, where the bathroom and front room were located. The empty area where the kitchen had once stood was in major disrepair, and the front room, with its leaking roof and broken floorboards, was a bare shell. The bedroom, separated by a few steps from the front room, was on the top floor. We sometimes laughed as the ceiling was so low we had to bend slightly to avoid hitting our heads.

From time to time, I would look through the tiny sash windows of the main room down to the bustling main road. There was never a dull moment in the area. The bus stop serving as a junction for several routes was situated directly outside the shop, so it was always full of lively conversation and a rush of people coming and going. While waiting for buses, people gazed through the shop window at the display of cakes, cheeses, pâtés, and other foods we had on show. Occasionally, they would run in to quickly buy a cake or ready-made sandwich to eat on the go.

We moved out of 181 into door number 275 on the 23rd of December and were relieved to have our own space again, even though the tiny bedroom was the only habitable space. Before we moved in, my husband spent time carpeting and decorating the room, and we managed to buy a small TV and a mobile gas heater to keep the room warm. It was the beginning of an exciting new start, and the front door key was our own. This ended another chapter in our lives and gave us a type of stability, although temporary. Locking the shop at the end of the day and rushing upstairs was a settling experience, and as we opened the door to the room at the top of the building, it welcomed us with warmth and the smell of newly laid carpet.

The Coldest Winter

That winter was one of the coldest. The little white van had broken down, leaving us to rely on public transport. There was no central heating in the apartment, so we lived out of the bedroom with the small Calor gas heater for warmth. We cooked our meals in the microwave in the shop, then after locking up, we climbed the stairs as quickly as we could to the room at the top of the apartment. That winter was harsh, but at that point, our relationship was calm for a while until the arguments started again and intensified. I spent a few nights at my sister Georgia's home, and after being encouraged, I would return home. Staying with family was probably not the best choice, but our marriage was deteriorating physically and verbally, and I simply needed to get away from the shop, customers, and my husband. The situation, despite efforts, was fast reaching its peak.

That Summer

That summer, I remember buying several stems of large white flowers, which I put in a glass vase and placed in the bathroom. Although the room was small, when we moved into the property, we discovered a large, original, free-standing Victorian rolltop bath with its four legs standing on the broken wooden floor. It was a luxury we enjoyed. Like a well-administered massage, it felt soothing to close my eyes at the end of the day, sink in, disappear into its depths amongst the bubbles, and forget the realities we faced. One morning, I sat in the bath and glanced over at the white flowers. As I looked on, it was as though they grew larger and appeared to glow brighter and brighter. It was then, in that instant, I knew.

The doctor's results confirmed I was pregnant. Despite the pregnancy not being planned, I was ecstatic beyond what I could have imagined, knowing I was going to have a baby after four bittersweet years of marriage. Now something amazing was happening to us. We hadn't planned to start a family, but I was now twenty-seven, moving toward thirty, and the biological clock had started ticking. Still, I remained focused on the plans we had made to develop the business.

I vividly recall the moment I told my husband. It was a hot day in July as we stood in the middle of the empty front room in the flat. The roar of traffic and the sound of conversations rose from the busy main road through the rickety window panes to fill the space prepared for the announcement. The sun was bright that day, and its rays hit the wooden floor as I nervously stood waiting to give him the news.

"The doctor has confirmed—I'm pregnant!"

My husband's reaction unfolded like camera stills displaying the picture and caption for each word as he first turned away to face the door and then returned to hug his wife, almost as an afterthought. His mixed emotions hung densely in the uncomfortable atmosphere. In that moment, my body received his embrace, but my mind sensed his feelings. Such was the intensity of that moment; his words were lost in the initial response.

We continued to struggle with very little money to meet business commitments, buy stock, and cover our own needs. Then to add a new mini but welcoming challenge, my senses aroused to protect the new temporary member of my body. Aromas I usually enjoyed, such as coffee and tea, now made me feel physically sick, as well as the smell of fried food. The hours I could spend working without tiredness reduced significantly, with my need to take frequent rests. It was all new to me, but like countless women, I didn't question the changes but accepted them as part of a natural course of events.

The drama slowly played out as we continued to fend off bailiffs from walking onto the shop premises to remove items from the business or personal belongings to clear our debts. One afternoon, as I was coming to the end of the first three months of the pregnancy, I left the shop to go upstairs to get some rest. I hadn't been sleeping for long when the room door opened, and looking up, I was shocked to see a tall, sturdy man standing in the doorway who I quickly realised was a bailiff. I heard the heavy steps of my husband chasing behind, who grabbed him and got into a short scuffle until the man backed down and left the room and shop premises without any of our belongings. We both realised then that it was no longer safe or comfortable for me to live at 275. That night we agreed I would stay with my parents and attempt to get re-housed by the local council.

The lowest and saddest point in our lives that summer witnessed an afternoon when we drove to South West London to get away from our miserable circumstances. Our dream was ebbing away, and we couldn't stop it. We drove down to the riverside full of parents and children with an ice cream van parked nearby. My husband asked me if I wanted an ice cream, which I did, and we spent a few moments counting the remaining coins we had between us, which was just enough for one to share. Despite how low we felt that day, we spent a peaceful moment together.

Back to Door 39

It felt strange yet comforting to be back at number 39, the place where I grew up with my siblings and the room where I slept with my two sisters. We were far away from the sound of traffic and loud conversations rising from the streets and seeping through the rickety Victorian sash bedroom windows at the top of the shop. Now, the only sounds I heard were birds chirping in the morning and the distant sound of an occasional car driving along the side road. Opening the bedroom window, I looked down into the garden where we had spent many years playing, etching our names as permanent reminders into the brick walls of our family home. Nothing much had changed in the room, only that my mother had made use of the space and filled the empty wardrobes with her clothes.

We had left home, and our parents were now discovering their new lives, becoming increasingly busy with church and travelling abroad. For the first few weeks, it felt good to be home, but as the moments passed, I had time to reflect on our lives and began to miss my husband. I filled my first week at the local housing office in an attempt to find a home, and the advisors made me aware that I would be entitled to a small amount of financial help.

Until this point, I had always worked, so I had no idea how the social system worked, and the aim was to find a job as soon as possible. Then, four months into my pregnancy, Father provided me with an opportunity to work not far from where I lived with a six-month contract. Although I wasn't able to continue to the end, the role was perfect. It was motivating and rewarding, and the team I worked with were innovative and inspiring. And above all, I was earning a regular income.

Father was showing himself as the Door to meet my needs through His Son Yeshua, with each door bringing the help I needed at each stage to meet the challenge. From door 2A to number 39, despite the experiences behind each door, there was an opportunity for change and development in my character, even though it felt as though my "building" was breaking down. Like the Woman in 31 working with "willing hands," Father was in my life to "work out his plans for my life" (Psalms 138:8) during what seemed like the darkest moments.

God is described as "light," and there isn't any darkness in Him, although at times it feels as though we're not seeing clearly. One night I dreamt I was walking on a very dark road, unable to see ahead, until I heard the words, "Turn on the lights." That specific light is called trust, being able to trust in Father who shows us that "there is no darkness in Him at all" (I John 1:5). He doesn't change with time.

Chapter 5

Discovering Your Strengths and Needs

HEY
**She is like the merchant ships,
bringing her food from afar.**

I had entered a new phase in my life that would slowly unfold over the next ten years. I believe the descriptions of the Woman in 31 show the different stages we revisit many times in our lives, like a circular event, with each experience bringing a new perspective and opportunities for Father to further develop, fine-tune, and strengthen our characters.

~

The Meaning of Hey

Linked to the fourteenth verse, the Hebrew letter *Hey* is the fifth letter in the alphabet with a numerical value of five. Interestingly, it appears twice in the Hebrew letters of God's name, pronounced by Christians as Jehovah or Yahweh.

However, Jews insert *Adonai* or *HaShem,* meaning "The Name." The four Hebrew letters in God's name are YHVH, which are as follows: "Y" pronounced as "yod" (rhymes with "mode"), "H" pronounced as "hay," "V" pronounced as "varv," and finally ending with the letter Hey. The meaning of the letters in God's name also reveals Jesus or Yeshua because the meaning of YHVH (Yod, Hey, Vav, and Hey) can be understood to mean "The revelation of the Hand and the Nail." The fifth letter of the Hebrew alphabet "H" for Hey speaks of "revelation," "production," and "new direction."

With every new life experience, we discover our strengths and needs while God constantly gives us insight (revelation) about ourselves, providing deeper perception of who we are. And as we journey through our lives, we are able to appreciate others in a better way. Our lives don't follow a linear pattern, meaning each experience is not "start," "finish," "next," and "never to re-visit again!" Each phase takes time as we go through the event and learn from it.

Imagine your process starting at one point on a circle and, later on, returning to the same point, adding another layer of learning and meaning to the experience. That point in the cycle is "Hey," a time of learning, being productive, and having the ability to see things clearly or follow a new direction. I'm not talking about a religious philosophy here, but following the lines of Hebraic thinking. Scriptures say, "History merely repeats itself. It has all been done before. Nothing under the sun is truly new" (Ecclesiastes 1:9).

Our lifelong learning follows these cycles, but at every point of learning and experience, the environment, events, and people will be different as God continues to build our character and offers another opportunity to learn and respond differently.

This is the reason I'm learning not to worry about experiencing what I call "I've been there before" situations because I understand that God is adding to what I have learned.

Let's revisit the fourteenth verse, which is linked to Hey:

"She is like the merchant ships, bringing her food from afar."

"Food," as denoted here, can represent many things. The challenge is you've got to know where to look for it. Without Father's revelation you can't find direction or be productive (i.e., "her food"), so the years pass. You may feel life is pretty mundane and filled with routine. I often say, "There is power in routine!" because it's the everyday life events where patterns of strengths, interests, and even passions are identified. For example, our daily interactions, conversations, and the ability to listen may indicate communication strengths. Following that path could open up possibilities such as coaching or training and more. We have to keep looking to God for His mind on the direction of our lives and do it continually. I encourage you to make a conscious effort to practice it regularly.

As my journey unfolded, I became increasingly unhappy, and my world was reduced to a small, locked room inside my head. However, I was yet to understand that this new road on my journey or point on the circle was less about productivity and more about following a new direction.

After many desperate attempts to keep the shop open my husband finally conceded to the fact that we could no longer keep the business afloat, and Benjamin's closed its doors on our dreams and efforts for the last time. While waiting for housing, my husband continued to live in the flat above the shop that he now shared with a group of young people of similar age who had been squatting. In exchange for a joint agreement for a temporary place to stay, they offered to help my husband manage the large, now-empty building. Looking back at this snapshot we would ordinarily never have experienced, that tough circumstance brought everyone together for a short while to share, support, and survive.

Summer had now ended, the nights were getting longer and cooler, and the utilities had now been cut, so there was no electricity in the building. Although I never saw how it was actually done, a few in the group had ways to "restore" the electricity. This gave us a few more months of lighting and the ability to prepare food in the small microwave. For a brief moment, it felt like we had been brought together, like Maslow's theory, to share a common need for shelter, warmth, food, and conversation.

Samuel

At number 39, I would lay on the bed trying to solve the problems we were facing, and then my thoughts would settle on the name we would call our child. One night as I was talking to God, I clearly heard "Samuel" and instantly knew that God had spoken. Wanting to hear my husband's choice, I decided not to share the name God had given to me and waited to listen to his thoughts.

I would stay at number 275 with my husband on the weekends, returning to my parents' home on Saturday evenings. During a weekend evening discussion, I asked him about the name we should give our child. He chose Samuel. This was a "Hey moment," a moment of revelation. That weekend I went back to my parents' home on a high, full of hope and encouraged to know God had not only given us a name for our child but was closely involved in the intricate details of our lives.

Living apart for five months allowed me time to think about the four tumultuous years we had spent together until this point. Admittedly, I guess I had more time to reflect since my husband was busy winding down the company. I'm sure he also used the time to reflect, and deciding whether to move forward with our marriage became another sharp, painful twist. Late summer into early autumn was filled with anxiety, waiting and hoping he would commit to giving us a second chance. Talking with my mother one afternoon, I was able to share my feelings and where my life was at that point. It was then she read the scriptures from Isaiah 45, "Sing oh childless woman...break into loud and joyful song...." It was the first time I read those words, and although I didn't fully understand it, I found them captivating and encouraging. They would stay with me for years to come.

As my mother read, she seemed to shape each word in her mouth before carefully releasing them:

"You will no longer remember the shame of your youth..."[1]

As she continued reading, and I immersed myself in her words, hope blossomed within me, and each word grew strong, leaping off the page with a seemingly three-dimensional presence.

"I will rebuild you on a foundation of sapphires."[2]

Afterward, I felt strong and ready to accept the fact that the

---

1. Isaiah 54:4 NLT
2. Isaiah 54:11 MSG

future may not take shape the way I wanted. I now understand that this prophetic book and chapter in Isaiah is multi-layered in meaning, but I grasped them on a concrete level relevant to my life. Years later I would experience the words "mountain of sapphires" in a way I'd find surprising.

I was enjoying my pregnancy, extremely happy and excited to know we were going to have a child. Even though at the time we were living apart, my husband took time from the business he was concluding to attend our first antenatal. The waiting area where I sat gave a clear view of the long clinical corridor to the hospital entrance, and I regularly glanced towards the door in anticipation of his arrival. After casting several furtive glances at people entering and leaving, the door finally opened, and this time he was there. I watched him walk hurriedly towards me with the same excitement and nervousness I felt, and during that moment, I believed there was still hope for us. As summer turned to autumn and the pregnancy progressed, my contentment increased while I waited for notice of our accommodation to come through, offering another chance to rebuild our home. However, I hadn't realised the profound impact the last few years had on our marriage and that we were having to rebuild our lives. We both had to want it. I certainly did.

Door 67

In the spring of the following year, we became proud parents of a wonderful baby boy. Our lives, nestled into our home at number 67 in East London, ran parallel to the closing down of our business affairs in South London. This door, number 67, opened to the happiest and most intimate moments of our marriage, providing further opportunity for a new direction and a longing for stability. We turned the key to the door of a ground-floor flat that had stood empty for some time and was in dire need of decoration. We later discovered the previous tenant was an elderly man who had lived there for many years. We never met the neighbour upstairs, but he made himself present through what sounded like heavy, painful bronchial coughing.

The ceiling in the main room was covered in the dark, yellow stain of a heavy smoker, and in the adjacent room, an old gas cooker sat in the corner on a crude kitchen floor in desperate need of tiles. The main living space was a fair size, and the square window framed the scenery to a small patchy grass area where the local dog owners exercised their pets. This area claimed the only green space amidst the concrete homes. At regular intervals the muted, low-pitched sound of the rusty gate bolts announced the entrance of the pet and its owner.

The kitchen window offered another perspective of the area as it overlooked the remainder of the council estate, which always looked grim, especially on grey rainy days. It was a sharp contrast to the leafy, green, affluent suburb where we had first started our lives. Despite everything, we were happy and content to rest in a new home, however temporary, while planning our next move.

A New Environment and Happy

Heavily pregnant, I continued to walk everywhere as the small white delivery van which we had used as a main form of transport had been stolen outside the flat one night. We actually heard the sound of the engine as it started, but as soon as my husband rushed to the window, the van was being driven at top speed down the street! We later found the vehicle abandoned not far from where we lived. The police informed us that it had been "borrowed" for criminal use. The van was the last attachment we had to Benjamin's Delicatessen. It wasn't funny then, but later we would laugh as we re-told the story.

Despite having no transport, I enjoyed riding around on buses and walked as much as I could to get maximum exercise. I tried to make sense of our new environment, even though everywhere was concrete and sterile compared to the lush green area where we had once lived. Our spirits remained high, nonetheless. Our son was soon due, we had a home that was stable and relatively safe, and we were making plans for the future. We were happy.

I found a local butcher who sold a selection of cooked meats and quality jams unusual for the area and decided to shop there as often as it provided a remote link to the "familiar." Other than the local shop visits, my journey would be to take a bus ride to the Marks and Spencer a few miles away, where I bought salads, desserts, and cold custards to satisfy my cravings while we waited for a second-hand cooker to arrive. Returning home, I would take the short walk through the concrete underpass that connected to the other side of the motorway leading to the apartment. This was a brief but depressing part of the day as the ground was always littered with rubbish, dog excrement, and saliva, the grimy tiled grey walls sprayed with graffiti, and the constant smell of urine filled the air.

I loathed this time but would cover the short walk as quickly as my eight-month belly and my shopping bags would allow, keeping my head down to avoid unpleasant deposits on the ground and eye contact with dubious individuals. I moved so fast, I almost glided over the ground until I opened the door at number 67 and stepped into the welcoming environment of the new home we had created. In the early evening, the underfloor heating would draw us into its warmth, and as the evening progressed the rooms would become progressively hotter until we would have to escape outside to breathe in the cold night air.

Leah

Two unexpected realities brought my youngest sister and me together. The first, happy moments, when, at different times, we announced our pregnancies to our parents. The second was painful events, which ached less as we shared our experiences. In many ways, our lives were mirror reflections at that stage. Even our first children were born within a week of each other! Leah's baby was born at the end of March, exactly a week ahead of mine, in the same hospital, and by April, we were both mothers.

Leah was to later bring the sparkle back into my life and show me how to live again. From the moment we reunited, after years of trying to frame and fill our lives, we discovered a new aspect of our sister relationship. Little did we realise that Father had strategically positioned us as gems in each other's lives to deal with the difficult days ahead.

God promises to work everything (in our lives) out for our good. We proved this to be true during a period of tough times when He did, in fact, work everything out well. We needed each other, and our many similar experiences brought our lives together, giving us our first major bond since leaving home.

Our lives, though filled with concerns, were happy times, and we met together as much as we could to chat, shop, and attend antenatal classes where we were taught strategies to help first-time mothers care for their newborns. One particular class we attended remains fixed in my memory.

A small group of women seated on chairs in a semi-circle fixed their gaze on the midwife using a life-size baby doll to demonstrate washing and feeding. I'm not sure what triggered the humour of that moment, whether it was something about the way the lifelike doll was being used or how the midwife handled it with such a serious facial expression. Perhaps it was because we enjoyed the midwife's demonstration with the doll. Maybe we were simply laughing at life! Whatever the reason, we looked at each other and, as if on cue, burst out laughing— discreetly at first, then loudly, and we just couldn't stop! And I mean it literally when I say we could not stop laughing!

It was both an embarrassing and hilarious moment. There we were, heavily pregnant, high on hormones, and we simply couldn't control ourselves. The midwife stopped her demonstration and glared at us with an accompanying parental-like frown that made us regain control and stop immediately. This was one day of many happy times we spent as expectant mothers, even though we were uncertain about what to expect amidst the tough circumstances we were facing.

Giving Birth

Giving birth to Samuel brought our lives into sharp focus. We were now proud parents, and the priorities we held as a young couple without children quickly readjusted. As is true of any first-time mum, it took a while for me to adjust to the new routine, but realising my time was no longer my own, I quickly transitioned into the new role and took pride in my baby son. My husband took to cycling to his new job in central London, allowing me to use the car during the day. And although he enjoyed the exercise, the long journey and the job, with its physically demanding hours, were exhausting. Arriving home, he would collapse onto the sofa, hold our son in his arms, and fall asleep. Even so, for the first time in years, we were spending evenings together and sharing a regular family routine in a safe place without intrusions.

Time and space had been created for us to enjoy those precious moments with our son, watching him grow into the first three months of his young life. It was like Father had given us this retreat to escape and rest from the madness of the last four years. When we closed the door to number 67, we shut out all the hurt, disappointment, tiredness, anger, and arguments from the past and locked ourselves into happier times, planning a new future. On New Year's Eve, we looked out into the night sky filled with sparkle, colour, shapes, and sounds from fireworks, bringing in the next year and a new door.

Change Arrived Early

Change arrived in the early summer that year and shifted us back to South London, an area we still affectionately called home. Although the people in the section of East London where we lived were generally friendly, the area was sometimes challenging. There was little quality of life in terms of open green spaces, shops, schools, and local recreation facilities; furthermore, my husband was keen to return to the familiar area of South London he had always known to start a business.

Soon after our son was born, he viewed a property on a small but fairly busy side road off a main high street in South East London. The road was home to a vibrant weekend farmers market selling all types of home-made foods, art, crafts and fashion. While I looked after our son, he was busy negotiating the lease and making financial arrangements to open up what would be the first reputable coffee shop in the local area.

Door 27A

The ground floor to door number 27A, our new home, was just a three-minute walk to the new business. We were allocated the property by the local council, and while temporarily living in East London, my husband spent evenings and weekends after work cleaning, decorating, and making it home. In July of that year, we were ready to move in, and it was time to leave the happy and close times we spent together as a family at number 67.

Moving brought mixed feelings. Door 67 had opened a place to recover and rest as a young family; there was a normality in the daily routine we had not experienced for years, and it was good for us. We had become friendly with a young man from Ghana who was new to the country and lived a few doors away. One morning, he knocked on the door to introduce himself. He explained he had noticed that the bottled milk the milkman left outside our door was being stolen as soon as the milkman left. A few weeks earlier, we had realised the milk had been disappearing but couldn't work out what was happening until one morning my husband managed to catch the person: a tall and lean older man, looking as though he was in need of a meal —and milk.

Similar aspirations drew my husband and our Ghanaian neighbour into long hours of conversation fuelled with business ideas and opportunities. As young people, we were hungry for change. Above all, beyond the meeting of minds, it was comforting to know that we were looking out for each other.

When we suddenly announced we were leaving, there was a look of sadness on his pleasant face. Still, he was happy for us, and when we left number 67, he watched and waved us goodbye. Little did I know, East London would soon draw me back.

Number 27A, the street door, led to a small entrance area with doors to both flats. The upstairs flat was owned by a man who was a musician. I would sometimes meet him at the main door and share a quick exchange of conversation pleasantries, but other than that we rarely saw him. Our front door opened up to a short and very narrow hallway with the front room and single bedroom immediately to the left. Due to lack of space in the flat, I usually folded my son's buggy and parked it in the communal entrance without objections from our neighbour. The hallway led to a kitchen with a wall separating the bathroom, which completed the space at the end of the property.

Short, Sharp, Shocks

Life at 27A became a series of short, sharp, painful shocks for a young mother. The desire to rebuild our lives through the business remained the gnawing hunger and determination that fuelled my husband. And to an extent, I understood, but it was one of two things: I could either keep up the pace or struggle behind with the distance increasing. The default was the latter.

When we moved into 27A, our son was around two and a half months, and I was a young mum with no immediate support physically, mentally, or emotionally. South London was quite a distance from East, and my sister, parents, and church community were no longer a short drive away. My husband spent up to twelve hours a day at the business, which was comparable to a needy young child. While I nurtured our baby son, he nurtured the business. I found myself becoming increasingly isolated, going long days without seeing friends or family and spending many evenings alone.

My close friend, Anna, now lived in South West London, and I could only make occasional visits. Attempting to make friendships, I joined a local mother and toddler group. Unfortunately, I would later discover that besides sharing similar experiences of being young mums, conversations didn't venture beyond the weekday group meeting. The toddler group was highly organised, and the "baby club committee" met once a month. It seemed, however, that the group was mostly made up of mothers intent on turning a relaxed group into "power board meetings," in addition to being very cliquey. I slipped away quietly.

Other than food shopping, I spent time taking Sam to the local park, which we both enjoyed. This was where I watched him practice his baby steps once I'd lifted him from the buggy onto the winding pathway. I saw the joy on his face and listened to his excitable early first sounds and single words as I fit his little legs, which filled the heavily padded all-in-one coat, into the wooden baby swings where I would push him backwards and forwards, higher and higher. The park covered a large area with a narrow stream that twisted and turned along the direction of the park, and on sunny days it was a pleasure to sit with Sam, feeding the ducks and watching the calm water.

The park café's benches were positioned along the grassy areas. It was here I did a lot of thinking about my life and the now miserable marriage that was fraught with arguments. But God was there in the unhappiest moments, and although I didn't always sense His presence, He definitely carried me and calmed my distressed mind. What I didn't realise, however, was the rate at which I was spiralling into depression—that is until I found myself wanting to extend the regular ten-minute routine appointments at the doctor's meant primarily for Sam's developmental checks and then experiencing a sinking feeling when I left knowing another lonely evening lay ahead.

Counting Doors

One afternoon, as I pushed my son in his buggy away from the park to start the half-hour walk home, I found myself obsessively counting the number of doors of the large, beautiful homes I passed. Not only was I counting the doors, but I was tossing my thoughts backwards and forwards as if trapped in a repeating debate about what colour front door I would choose. This empty repetition continued for what seemed like hours.

Laughable but serious, my mental health in those moments was disturbed as I slipped without support into my lonely, isolated world with many long hours available to fuel my unhappiness. Only the long moments in deep prayer and meditation freed and spared my mind from damage. On many occasions as I read the poetic Psalms, God spoke to me through His Word, and I always remembered the promise my mother read during my stay at number 39: "I will rebuild you on a mountain of sapphires."

The arguments surfaced, stayed, and escalated, and with it, damaging words and harmful events. I began to loathe myself. I despised my reflection in the mirror, my weight, and lack of direction; my self-esteem was low, the relationship was crushing, and above all, I craved my husband's love and attention. I would often walk the short distance to the shop just to be close to him; admittedly, this was his focus and place of work. Everyone wanted his time—customers, suppliers, and staff, and the young business demanded time, a lot of it. I absolutely adored my time with my son, but I wished the days had allowed me the mental space to enjoy the early days to years with him that I would never have again.

Later that year, five months into Sam's first year, we discussed my return to work as finances were tight. This marked the beginning of a string of jobs to bring in extra income, first in a local bakery, then in a newly opened prestige bakery in a top London store in Knightsbridge. However, I did so reluctantly, and I'm not ashamed to say so. At that stage, I felt my son was too young to leave with childminders, and my heart was heavy with sadness. In addition to this, I was dealing with what I now understand was post-natal depression, but I had tried to bury it in shame, silent tears, and the belief that my behaviour was a sign of weakness. I didn't realise what was happening, and my husband couldn't see. But God knew, and despite all of this, He still held me on the same level as the 31 Woman and remained the Aleph, the strong leader of "Beyt," my life, and my shattering mind. Then one evening after working through two childminders, I walked the usual long route from the train station to the second childminder's home to collect Sam.

Still Visible

It was a cool early autumn late afternoon, and the falling leaves were gathering in an array of golds and browns on the ground. Locked in my own world, I lowered my head and swept them aside with long strides in a relaxing, sensory experience as I walked to pick up my son. It was now dark, and as I watched the ground move along beneath my steps, I came to a side road and stopped to allow the cars right of way. I raised my head briefly to notice a large, shiny, black, expensive sports car purposely slow to a stop for me to cross. I glanced to the right and noticed the driver was Lennox Lewis, a famous British boxer. He smiled and gestured with his hands for me to cross. Drained, with no make-up, and my dark blue wool coat wrapped around my body with the collar up for warmth, I quickly looked away, wondering why he had stopped his car for me to cross when it was his right of way. Later, reflecting on that moment, I believe Father was demonstrating that although I had lost myself, I remained fully visible and beautiful to Him.

I finally arrived at the house and knocked on the door, which the childminder's daughter opened. What followed next broke my heart. As I looked for my son, I discovered him crawling on the floor of a dimly lit room, brightened only by the light of a small TV. It wasn't that my son was being mistreated because I knew he was in good hands, but those hands weren't mine. As soon as he saw me, he cried, and it took some time to comfort him. I was devastated. It was then, at that moment, I decided not to return to work. I wasn't ready, and neither was he. This was my time to be with my son, and, looking back, I still don't regret the decision. I bundled my son in his buggy, and we started the long walk home, braving the brisk autumn wind.

Explanations

Explaining the events to my husband would prove to be the toughest part. He was furious and adamant that I needed to work, and I was determined that, at this stage, I would not. It was a stalemate. I knew that he was trying to push us forward, but at what cost? The months that followed were punishing for both of us until, finally, during the summer of the following year, I secured an administrative role at a central government office in the city.

Unlike my previous roles, the hours were nine to five, and I found local childminders—a husband and wife—for my son. They were an older couple, and I had a good feeling about their ability to look after Sam and provide the stimulation he needed. Starting work again filled me with hope, and I believed my relationship with my husband would improve. But to my disappointment, things didn't improve. In fact, things continued to deteriorate as I battled through my depression, shedding countless tears along the way.

As with any working parent, mornings were busy. One morning in particular, I left home having dropped my son off at the childminders only to realise, as I walked quickly to the bus stop, that I hadn't pulled up the zip of my skirt! It was a crazy situation. My husband and I were both usually busy in the mornings, but unlike our newly married lives at 2A, we were together yet separate. We no longer saw each other.

Leaving

One Saturday morning, I woke up crying. My whole world seemed as though it was caving in. The day before, I went to the surgery to see the doctor, but I just couldn't find the courage to explain how I was feeling. Feeling embarrassed, I left the building, dragging all the pain and darkness with me. Looking over at Sam sleeping in his cot positioned along the wall of our small bedroom kept me steady, and I prayed for courage to start the morning.

My marriage had completely broken down, and there was silence in the home. We couldn't communicate, and when we did, the words and actions were damaging. At some point that day, I decided to walk the short distance to the shop just to see him. I needed his reassurance that he still loved me; I wanted him to tell me that everything would be okay, but it was clear that our time together was fast coming to a close. I sat Sam in his buggy and walked to the shop. The defining moment that would alter the course of my life would be my husband's reaction. As I stood in the kitchen doorway, it appeared he completely ignored me as I lingered, desperate for his affection. I cried inside as I watched him walk towards our son, pick him up, and cuddle him. Then, just like that, he turned away and walked back into the kitchen.

Maybe I wasn't listening carefully to what Father was saying, but that moment of despair silently signalled the end of our marriage. I walked back to the flat, confused and rejected, and sat in the tiny front room looking at the walls, crying, feeling anxious, and wondering who I could call for support. There was no one. I was now screaming inside, so I called the doctor and demanded that she come to my home, but she suggested I go into the surgery. I insisted that I was in no state to leave the house, so she agreed to do a home visit.

The doorbell rang, and for that second, my body felt a surge of relief that someone was there to help. I opened the door to the young female doctor. The expression on her face reflected deep concern. She apologised repeatedly and then attempted to help me explain the surface of my drowning feelings. I recall fragments of the conversation:

"Hi, how can I help you?"

"Doctor, I can't stop crying. I feel lost, and I've no energy to do anything for myself or my son."

She asked me to explain further, and I skimmed through a brief description of my marital problems.

"Have you considered counselling?" she asked, the concern in her voice evident. "It may help you work through your feelings."

I admitted I hadn't but would be open to trying.

As the conversation came to an end, she suggested I see a counsellor at the surgery as early as Monday morning, and she would book the appointment. The doctor had now realised I needed help.

This was the lowest point in my life, and at no stage could I ever have compared myself to the 31 Woman. In sharp contrast to this Woman, I considered myself a failure. God, however, did not hold the perspective of my thoughts. He explains, "'My thoughts are nothing like your thoughts,' says the Lord. 'And my ways are far beyond anything you could imagine. For just as the heavens are higher than the earth, so my ways are higher than your ways and my thoughts higher than your thoughts.'" (Isaiah 55:8–9).

God holds time in front of Him. On one page, He sees my eternity past, eternity present and eternity future. At that moment—the moment of my deep despair—He saw my eternity present and future, a woman with a character to build, a woman who would later pour His love into the lives of countless others. At that moment, however, I didn't see that woman; I couldn't see a future except the pain and failure of the present and the fear of the future. Then I looked over at our beautiful son, and my hope was renewed, at least for a few hours.

The doctor's visit left me feeling safe in my mind for a short while, but it didn't last because as the Saturday afternoon turned into evening, waves of desperation swept in until I snapped, realising that the relationship had ended. A desperate call followed to my brother, the one who, four years earlier, had escorted me down the church aisle to meet the man I was now running away from.

John arrived to drive me away in his small bottle-green Mini Cooper. He had always been there for me even though we spoke infrequently. He pulled up outside the apartment and helped place two black bags of clothes and a few items I had collected—all that remained of my married life—into the tiny boot, with the third bag on the back seat. I sat in the back with Sam in my arms as my brother drove us through the South London streets into the cold night towards an uncertain future. But unlike the wedding, this event wasn't planned. He had to stop at a friend's home, and I waited in the car for a short while, giving me time to think about Monday morning.

I'm not sure where this fits in the Woman in 31's journeys except to say that the events in the shop and the doctor's home visits swept in a new season of change and direction. They would force me to push through fear and trust God completely. The early days of the new start at number 67 brought hope but soon faded as the new stage pushed a young family into areas we were unprepared for with no appreciation or discussion of the pressures it would bring. During this time, I continued to pray however I could and drew hope from His encouraging words I read when times seemed darkest.

Chapter 6

Staying Connected in Tough Environments

VAV
It's still dark when she rises to give food to her household and orders the young women serving her.

No Valentine

The home where I had grown up seemed to illuminate the dark, wet February night as my brother's Mini pulled up outside. I thought I'd be alone in the maze of what had just happened. But once again, on that unplanned weekend, lives that somehow mirrored each other brought my sister Leah and her baby daughter back to the room we left. Circumstances had reconnected two sisters, now two women with grown-up stories to tell of lives that appeared broken. Back in the bedroom overlooking the garden where we had grown up, we now hugged and looked at our babies as we talked about our lives and how events would unfold the next day on Monday morning, our first Valentine's Day as single mothers.

~

The Meaning of Vav

Linked to the fifteenth verse, *Vav*, the sixth letter of the Hebrew alphabet, strongly hints at Jesus or Yeshua. Primarily, the letter is associated with the word "nail," as its purpose is to connect. It was the three-quarter-inch-thick and seven-inch-long nails driven into his wrists and feet that brutally connected Jesus, Yeshua, to an olive and acacia wood cross where He willingly gave up His life and bled for my haemorrhaging life. He suffered and felt the pain for all lives.

This "nail" connected with the pain of the loneliness I was experiencing on an entirely different level as I transitioned into the role of a mother bringing up her son alone. At the same time, Vav connected me to the healing that gradually came as I determinedly pushed forward to complete the words of the prophet in Isaiah chapter 53, verses 4 and 5, where it reads, "In fact, it was [my] diseases He bore, [my] pains from which He suffered; yet [I] regarded him as punished and afflicted by God. But He was wounded because of [my] crimes, crushed because of [my] sins; the disciplining that makes [me a] *whole* [*woman*] fell upon him, and by his bruises (or in fellowship with him) [I] am healed" (CJB). I have personalised this verse, which is how I sometimes read the powerful words, making them become vibrant, three-dimensional, and more meaningful to my life.

This part of my journey was about experiencing my faith in 3D. The fragments of my life slowly came together as I connected with God in a concrete way, which showed He was walking alongside and connecting with me at every step. As I began to understand how He worked in my life, my trust grew stronger. I realised that as well as walking next to me, He was walking way ahead to clear the way for the next day of my future.

"Darkness" (in verse fifteen) describes the sometimes-tough environment in which women, like the Woman in 31, provide for their homes whilst managing every area of their lives. How many times have we watched interviews or read profiles of women who seem to have an admirable balance in their lives? CEOs are seemingly able to juggle motherhood, relationships, and work. The mother who prepares super home-cooked meals, manages school runs and homework, organises outside activities for the kids, and is perfectly groomed, all while maintaining a stable and happy household with her husband. The woman who has moved from education into a long-desired career or the woman able to balance business and family. Really? No, I don't think so.

We know it's the glimpse of an outsider looking in, but the truth is that women are finding strategies, coping through various means, and creating supportive or coping mechanisms to make their lives run while they are the steel pin for everyone else. This woman needs strength from somewhere to balance her life and family, and she will source it from whatever provides the emotional, mental, physical, and spiritual recharge she needs. The strength of the Woman in 31 comes from God, the Aleph, who has everything she needs.

"And the church is his body; it is made full and complete by Christ, who fills all things everywhere with himself."

—**Ephesians 1:23**

We are "His body." Christ makes us, the Woman, full and complete. He fills our lives with Himself.

The powerful image presented for this Woman can only exist as she depends on Father, the Strong Leader (Aleph) of her life (Beyt). As He gives her what she needs (Gimel), she then enters the door (Dalet) to become productive (Hey) and connected to His Son Yeshua (Vav). She is able to dig deep into God to support her human spirit, emotions, and body by His Spirit and to give inner peace and balance. Otherwise, outside of that, she relies on other structures. The wise woman builds her house, life, "Beyt," on a rock-solid foundation with the assurance that He cares for the whole woman.

Staying Afloat

I was kept afloat by two amazing women who worked in my office and support from my sister and aunt, and I'll describe how, later, God provided the perfect daycare setting for my son. In the small accounting office where I worked, one of the two women was the supervisor. She was warm, caring, almost motherly. Although she had a lot going on in her own life, she was always available to listen. My other colleague listened with endless patience as I poured out my problems whenever we went to lunch. Despite the heavy workload, those were the times when taking an hour for lunch was the norm, so we took advantage of every minute.

When the weather was pleasant enough, we would stroll down London's famous Chancery Lane, lined with its large mature trees, restaurants, and sandwich shops constantly filled with the flow of bustling lunchtime crowds. On warmer days we would divert to the famous street market, passing a well-known Italian delicatessen with the largest choice of olives I had ever seen and an impressive array of wines. I imagined myself one day with a large budget walking in and buying as many varieties of olives, wine and bottles of first-pressed olive oil. The vibrant city street market was continually packed with lunchtime shoppers stopping to snap up a bargain from the many stalls selling clothes and household items. The air was always filled with the wafting aroma of fresh, savoury, and sweet foods being cooked to serve the hungry. Within that rich environment, I recharged, chatted and listened to advice from my friend. At the end of the month, on payday, Friday's plans were usually made for the small accounts office to take a joint lunch, and this was enough to keep my social life afloat and help maintain some normality.

Shelter

The first week back at number 39 was challenging, and my energies were focused on finding a place for Sam and me to live, along with suitable daycare. Despite having a young baby of her own, Leah willingly offered to look after Sam during the day, sharing the responsibility with my aunt, who lived nearby. Knowing my family was looking after Sam was a great relief. Leah's and my situation was described as "homeless from home." This definition was the label qualifying us to apply for social housing, and for myself, it was the second time in my life I "wore the label" since losing the business and returning to my parent's home.

The process was slow, agonising, and close to soul-destroying as, yet again, I was at the local housing office, having to join long queues of people in desperate need of somewhere to live.

The many hours I sat waiting were spent praying for stability in my life. I quickly worked out that this process required patience and resolved to wait. I would sit and people-watch, wondering about their journeys and what brought them to this stage. My thoughts were usually interrupted by the harsh sound of my name being called over the loudspeaker, followed by the instruction to go to the available room where the housing officer waited to see the next number from the long line of the homeless.

Stressful conversations took place in dreary, grey booths where I had to be prepared to reveal every area of my private life, financial affairs, and inevitably, my emotions to someone who would rarely raise their head except for a furtive glance to check if the number they had called was still, sitting in front of them. Like many, I was another number and name on a long list of people to see that day. At times, it felt humiliating. However, despite the grim nature of a necessary process, there was always a glimmer of hope I would find somewhere to live. So I trusted Father, the Aleph, the Strong Leader of my life, to lead me on this new road.

A Yellow Happy House

Almost a month after I had returned home, and at one of my lowest points, my emotions raw and bare, I wrote, "...my life is a mess." Two days later, I followed up with a call and an appointment to see a woman who ran a daycare centre from her home. A small, yellow house with a multicoloured hand-painted nursery sign reading Cheeky Cherubs in the ground floor front window appeared to dance and welcome me.

I had a good feeling about the woman called Sue from the moment she opened the door. She was warm and friendly with a large smile and mid-length, fine bleached-blond hair sitting on her shoulders. It was as though she had been waiting for me for a long time. We talked, and she straightaway offered a space for Sam, two days at first, until the summer when a few children were due to move to school.

I noticed the house's ground floor had been converted into a nursery that had planning permission to care for up to seven preschool-age children. A week later Sam started nursery, and once he got through his morning protest screams at being left, he quickly settled. I would return in the evening to a happy and contented little boy who would have stayed longer.

Fridays at the nursery signalled a welcome end to the week and was always filled with the strongly scented aromas of home cooking. Geoff, Sue's husband, loved to cook, and weekends were when they made a special effort to scan recipes for new meal ideas and relax together. There was time to discuss food and wine, and it was the time when Geoff let us into the kitchen and gave his secret recipe for spaghetti bolognese, which later became Sam's favourite meal. Watching this couple gave me hope that relationships could be happy and that one day I would find my own. Father found a place for Sam, and that settled my main anxiety as I was constantly aware my sister had similar issues and needed time and space to work out her own life. I will always ever be grateful to Leah for her support.

This part of my life was about staying connected in dark times and at all times. It's about Father connecting me to Himself by holding my hands tightly, even though I didn't always feel He was there. I have learned that walking with Father is not about feelings but trust. It's about God connecting me with Himself, time, people, and life.

Keys

Two months after my sister and I had returned home, on the 2nd of April, I received a letter from the council to say they had allocated me a temporary property and requested I collect the keys a few days later. That weekend I was excited at the prospect of a new home, however temporary. I took a day's leave, and Leah and I went to view the place. What we saw was depressing. Later that evening I wrote in my diary, "The property was awful, located in some forsaken area on the outskirts of London. It was the epitome of my worst domestic nightmare." As we looked around the dark, ground-floor flat, the carpet was thick with ground-in food, stains of different kinds, and what looked like syringes in the corner of the main room. My heart sank lower than the filthy floor, and my sister insisted that we leave and look no farther. I listened and followed her out.

That afternoon I returned the keys to the Homeless Person's Unit (HPU), as it was called then, but not without having to give a full explanation of the reasons I was unable to take the property. The officer, though sympathetic, advised that under council policy, I would only be offered a second property, after which, if I did not accept, they would take the opinion that I made myself "intentionally homeless" and would no longer be eligible for housing. Despite the disappointment, my sister's strength that day was the rock I needed.

The weekend passed with us indulging in films I had missed over the years, Leah bringing me up to date. She introduced me to video shops, and we rented enough films to last the weekend. I was absorbed in my movie "catch-up," watching the latest by Spike Lee and others. It took our minds off the bitter situation that threatened to crush our hope but for the love of Abba Father and His clear, stable steps in our messy lives.

A week later I collected the keys for a second property, this time less excited and more cautious of what lay behind the door. My subsequent diary description read, "Horrible. Lots of roaches. Work needed. I'm confused and unhappy. I just want to cry. Where next?" I returned to work around midday, in time for Friday's regular end-of-month office lunch filled with laughter and comfort food in a Chancery Lane Brasserie. This was just the medicine I needed. Looking back, I was never quite sure how all the Friday afternoon work got done after a long lunch and heavy stomachs, but it did, somehow.

What Next and Where Next?

On Saturday morning, I enrolled in a local pottery class that offered childcare, where Sam could stay during my lesson. Learning pottery was the sensory and visual stimuli I needed. It allowed me time to think, and while I clumsily yet determinedly learned how to shape the pot on the rotating wheel, Father was shaping our lives, Sam's and mine, at the same time.

Chapter 7

Facing Life with Confidence

ZAYIN
**She considers a field and buys it, and
from her earnings she plants a vineyard.**

And so began a new chapter in my life, raising Sam and learning to love and live. With the prospect of social housing now over, I had no option but to rent privately. The problem was the large deposit I needed to raise from my small salary and little savings. Despite the hurdle, I decided to start the search and trust Father would work everything out.

Many property searches later, I found door 39. I was about to find out that this new road would bring me a glimpse of what God says in Jeremiah 29, verse 11: "For I know the plans I have for you says God, plans for well-being, not for bad things, so that you can have a hope and a future." (Jeremiah 29:11 CJB).

~

The Meaning of Zayin

Zayin, the seventh letter of the Hebrew alphabet, is linked to the sixteenth verse, "she considers a field and buys it, and from her earnings she plants a vineyard." The meaning of the letter Zayin is primarily "weapon" or "sword." The book of Hebrews chapter 4 describes Father's Word as "the sword of the Spirit," which can be seen as protective as we speak His powerful Words over our lives. Also, in the book of John, Jesus is known as "the Word."

A verse in the scriptures affirms God's words as "powerful," comparing them to the sharpness and precision of a sword but with the super ability to cut through the subconscious mind to reveal the thoughts we hide even from ourselves! Connected to the Father through Yeshua, I was able to allow His "sword" to cut through the knots in my life. Time and events proved this to be true, and his Words, like Zayin depicts, protected me on many occasions from being crushed under the pendulum swings of my emotions and their decisions.

This verse introduces the Woman's vineyard, and the perspective here is one of the Woman being productive. For me, this stage came later, as this time was about making sense of my life before I could even begin to plant. God's directions always came before I was about to derail plans with bad decisions based on raw, unaddressed feelings of rejection, loneliness, and an almost consuming need to be loved.

The number for Zayin is seven. It is biblically significant and is the number of completion. God rested on the seventh day as His Work was complete. This next stage in my life, though painful and sometimes dark, proved His words dependable and true. I can only describe this by saying that each letter formed words, and those words gave meaning that shaped my experiences when, at times, God used His Word like a sword to separate good from negative decisions. In the New Testament, Peter, one of Jesus' close followers, used his sword in a violent act. But in a swift compensatory action, Jesus healed the victim. Jesus is the Word and Sword in human form, and the purpose of the Sword was to show people that they needed answers only He could bring into their lives.

~

Door 39

I sat in the car on a road not far from the home I was about to view. It had the identical door number as the one where I grew up, 39. I waited, wondering whether this place would finally be the home I'd been looking for. Immediately and with clarity, I heard Father's voice.

"Go on. He's waiting for you!"

I can only describe it as a strong yet gentle voice that suddenly broke through my thoughts, instantly making me feel more at ease about the upcoming meeting.

The apartment was in a newly built block, located on the first floor on a quiet cul-de-sac opposite a large grassy mound, making the place feel secluded and tucked away from the world. It was the perfect location and would provide a welcome feeling at the end of the day. Turning the keys in the ignition of my red Fiesta, I drove up, parked in front of the small block, and looked up at the apartment.

I'll never forget the landlord's name, Mr. Warmisham. He became the first of many landlords I would have over the years.

I guessed he was in his late twenties—maybe early thirties—dark brown curly hair and a distinctive, gentle face. He smiled as we shook hands, then led me through the fair-sized rooms. The many windows shaded with blinds gave the living room a bright and airy feel, leading into the main living area where a black two-seater cloth sofa was the focal point.

A small side window in the living room overlooked the private carpark with allotted spaces. The dark green patterned curtains in the main bedrooms were made from heavy fabric, and a patterned blue covered the windows in the second bedroom. The bathroom floor was laid in marble with new appliances and held all the appeal of a modern bathroom. Under my feet the soft, new ivory carpet was the final invitation to sign the contract.

I had a feeling of peace and excitement and visualised myself living in what felt like a two-bedroom haven with its marbled bathroom and large kitchen-diner split living room. We ended the meeting with another handshake, the agreement made, and Sam and I were about to start a new life in a lovely home. I owe much thanks to my younger brother Don for having found the large deposit after walking in on me crying one evening when he came over to visit our parents. When he asked what was wrong, I managed a tearful explanation, to which he immediately responded, "Don't cry. I'll give you the money you need!" That's how God showed me He was walking ahead and alongside me. I will forever be grateful to Him, my parents, and my siblings for all the support they selflessly gave Sam and me during those years.

God's Zayin, His Word and "sword" in my life, was about to cut through and challenge perceptions about what I thought I could or couldn't change. I began to understand when I read

His written words, listened to the right advice from friends and family, and experienced everyday life events on "Monday morning," a phrase I use to describe the routine of life.

During our time at 39, Sam developed from a toddler to a five-year-old, and we had a lot of fun! Our weekends were usually filled with activities such as visits to some of London's famous tourist attractions like the science and history museums. We both enjoyed those visits as they involved underground train journeys to busy Kensington and Knightsbridge in West London, midday lunches, and long days ending with tired but satisfying trips home where we would return exhausted and content. Then there were the weekly food shops and visits to Leah's home, where Sam played with his little cousin, and Leah and I would talk for hours.

Our church community became a major lifeline with the older women mothering Sam, allowing time to rest my mind, exhale or teach at my father's request. Sunday afternoons were usually spent having lunch with Leah at our parents' home or dinner with friends. This is how I filled my weekends, which helped manage the loneliness I sometimes felt. During those two and a half years, I sampled a variety of evening courses, including counselling, photography, and Bible. This was also a way to meet new people and make friends. Above these activities, I was enjoying time with my son. However, once Sam was tucked away in bed, or those weekends came when he spent valuable time with his dad, I was alone and forced to face the overwhelming surge of loneliness and the grief of the demise of a marriage.

Weekends

The alternate weekends my son spent with his dad always opened at scene one of my emotional drama. Despite the predictable end, this drama played out perfectly every time, with me seemingly unable or not wanting the narrative to change.

My heart would beat knowing that shortly we would meet. My stomach churned with anticipation and excitement. Hair, makeup, and clothes would be perfect to present the emerging "new woman." I carefully packed the tiny clothes for my baby son in preparation for the short weekend with his dad.

The new apartment, pristine and manicured, gleamed with polished furniture positioned in hoovered, deep-pile ivory carpet. At a set time in the morning and afternoon, the sun's rays beamed through the large windows, giving a natural, golden warmth to the apartment. The artificial heat from the radiators in the winters could not compete.

I created this holistic environment as a package containing his son and his wife, a gift I hoped he could not ignore. Then, I waited, watching the agreed-upon time for his arrival pass slowly on the clock as the sun's rays faded.

This latter part of the 1990s was the beginning of the growing technology revolution. So, with only the house phone available to call his business, there was no other way to check whether his father had started the long journey across London.

The doorbell would finally ring, and despite the lengthy wait time, I presented calm and undisturbed yet, below the iceberg, brewed a mixture of annoyance and excitement amidst a longing to "talk" and "resolve" our problems. This scene never ended well. The conversation in scene one always took place in the hallway.

"Hi. You ok?" I would ask.

"Yes, fine," followed by an occasional peck on the cheek from him.

"How's the business?" started the second round of pleasantries.

"Oh, busy," with the usual complaint of staffing problems tagging the reply.

A loving big hug for our son was always warming for me to observe whilst handing over his weekend bag.

"Would you like some coffee?" I would ask, hoping he would stay for a bit longer.

"Thanks, but no. I've got to get back."

Back where? Where would he want to be but here with his only son and beautiful wife? Then the suppressed excitement would turn to disappointment, low self-esteem, tears, and the thought of a lonely weekend without my son.

The final act of the scene never changed. It involved me watching him strap our son in the car seat. After hugging my son and agreeing on a set time to return on Sunday, the front door closed, and the scene ended with me standing by the window, watching them disappear into the ever-increasing distance between us.

It was as though I was in the audience watching the same characters, scenes, and carefully rehearsed script play out with precision with full knowledge of how each scene would end. Even though the rift between my former husband and me had widened, our focus on life had diverged, and there were the realities of third parties, I buried those troubling thoughts. I believed I wanted our relationship to heal, or perhaps it was the "familiar" I craved. Whichever, the feeling was raw. I missed the fact that my son didn't have his dad present every day in the home. Having tried in vain to forget the painful, not-so-distant past and the fact that nothing had changed, I began to miss him for Sam—and for me.

As part of the fortnightly free performance, I would look out for his car to pull up outside the flat. I would stand by the window as Sam was comfortably strapped in his car seat and watch the car disappear into the distance and then wonder how I was going to fill the weekend in a beautiful but empty apartment. Then on Sunday night, I would wait with anticipation for my son and his dad to arrive. I repeated this crazy, self-tortuous routine for around three years, on and off, silently beating and tormenting myself with delusional ideas of mutual feelings— that he would look at me and want me in the same way. That time did arrive, but after years of destructive mind games, my thinking was changing about myself and the direction my future would take. Sunday evenings were the most painful times as I would wait for him to return with Sam and hope that after our brief chat, he would stay. It never happened, and when he left, I would cry inconsolably.

One night as I lay in my bed, exhausted from crying and trying to get to sleep, I could hear Sam turning about in his bed, unable to settle. Before going to his room to check on him, I paused in a moment of spontaneous prayer.

"God, if you hear me and are really in this situation with me, then please help Sam go to sleep."

And I'm not exaggerating, within a few seconds, there was quiet. I immediately went to his room to check if he was okay, and there he lay, sleeping soundly. This was another seemingly small but significant example of the many occasions where I proved for myself that Father was deeply involved in every area of my life, showing me that He was there with us both. Over the years, His Words became concrete in many situations, too many to write, and they were not coincidental but a reminder of His promise in the book of Isaiah: "When you go through deep waters, I will be with you. When you go through rivers of difficulty you will not drown." (Isaiah 43:2).

Turning 30

On my 30th birthday, I woke crying, weighed down by a mix of bleeding emotions. On the one hand, I experienced the joy of being a mum to my beautiful young son—on the other, the pain of watching my life and his unfolding without a husband and a dad. I needed him for Sam, yet I was afraid to accept the marriage was in pieces, and my feelings masked in loneliness were betraying realities that life had moved on.

My loving parents did the best they could and took me out to dinner at the local Chinese restaurant where, in between conversations, I sat watching the tropical fish dart around in a large tank. They mirrored my thoughts and feelings swimming around in a tank of emotion.

My late twenties and very early thirties were open for the Zayin, God's sword, and Father cutting away the old from the new and guiding me away from the destructive relationships that came. I was thirty, young, beautiful, ambitious, yet vulnerable. But what saved me from more disaster was God, who remained the Aleph, the Strong and Powerful Leader of my life, Beyt.

Education

After three years living at number 39, a change of direction came. I decided it was time to leave my mundane job as an administrative officer where, having moved from Chancery Lane in Central London, I had taken a job in a local housing office. Amazingly, after giving my employer notice I was leaving, I realised it had been exactly one year to the date I joined the company, and on a hot August summer's day, over a lunchtime meal in a garden restaurant, my colleagues wished me well. Later that week, as I was walking down the office to my desk carrying a large pile of files, I tried to steer out of the direction of a woman walking towards me. As she approached, she stopped and mentioned she had heard news of me leaving.

"I heard you were leaving," she said, forcing me to slow my gait. How will you manage to eat on a student income?" she almost sneered.

I calmly but emphatically replied, "Beans on toast!" and continued towards my desk without a break in my stride.

The decision was made. Years later, having qualified as a speech and language therapist, I met the same woman by chance on a busy street, and as we looked at each other in a brief exchange, her eyes seemed sad. Still employed with the company, she admitted she would have loved to have made a similar change to her life but was unable due to family and financial commitments. Whereas I had an opportunity and took it. That day I began a long journey to learning ways to allow God to help me look behind the behaviours women present. In some cases, including my own, women mask their true emotions and real thoughts. Only God's Word, represented as a sword symbolised by Zayin, is able to cut through our lives and into the hidden issues.

Change became the single constant in my life. It was bold, consistent, reliable, like a close friend, and, in a strange way, I depended on it as an indicator of progress in my life. The area where we lived was quickly deteriorating, and I began to feel unsafe. A few of the neighbours who had lived alongside for those three years had recently announced they were making plans to move. Like the woman in Proverbs 31, verse 16, it was time for me to plan for the future, and the next move was university. But before the days at 39 ended, Andrew entered my life.

Chapter 8

Embrace New Beginnings

CHET
She gathers her strength around her and
throws herself into her work.

When I first moved back home, five months pregnant, my mother showed me the written promises in the scriptures from Isaiah 54, which are multi-layered in meaning. Like most verses, we can apply those promises to our lives, for example, the words that promise, "I will build you on a mountain of sapphires." This was the first time I discovered those words, and occasionally I would sense a strong application of that promise in my life. Those words became a fence to block worrying thoughts, feelings of rejection, low self-esteem, and at times, depression.

Andrew

My eight—my new beginning—came with water. The house phone rang, and I picked up to hear Leah's voice. As I walked into the bedroom to talk, a long sister conversation about life began. Sam was spending the weekend with his dad, so there was a lot of time. I can't remember how long we'd been talking when the conversation was interrupted by several knocks at the front door. I put the phone down and opened the door to my neighbour, a tall man looking down at me with a noticeably kind face and warm smile.

A few Fridays previous, we met by chance at the main entrance to the building while collecting takeaways that had arrived at the same time. We exchanged brief introductions, and before I could politely refuse, he paid for the meal. Grateful, I thanked him and rushed up the stairs to eat and watch a film with Sam. I later found out he had recently moved into the ground-floor apartment. So, there he was, standing in the doorway with a kind but concerned look, asking me if I was okay. I can't remember the reason, but I felt slightly irritated at having my conversation with Leah interrupted. At the same time, I couldn't help but wonder why he knocked. He then explained water had started to leak lightly and then heavily from the ceiling light in his front room. I immediately realised what had happened! Apologising repeatedly, I left him standing at the front door and dashed into the kitchen.

Before my sister called, I had started to fill the kitchen sink with water to wash up and forgot. The floor was now deep in water as I rushed to close the tap. Then with a few steps to the front door, I gave a quick, embarrassed explanation, punctuated with apologies. He, however, just wanted to find out if I needed help, which I politely refused. When I asked about the extent of water in his apartment, he assured me everything was fine, and a few days later he reported. Thankfully, there was no damage.

That was the first of many brief introductions to Andrew. We met occasionally at the communal entrance or the local supermarket. One early summer morning, in the City of London, I noticed his tall frame walking towards me on his journey to work in the opposite direction, but that's as far as it went. Sometimes I would overhear part of his phone conversations as he paced about on the grassy bank opposite the building to get a better signal. Then one Sunday afternoon, he attended a service at my church wearing a bright lime green shirt, which I, or anyone else, couldn't miss. I looked around thinking, *There's my neighbour!* A friend at the time took to calling him "lime green," which I found amusing.

Around two years later, our brief meetings with polite social conversations meandered into friendship. The comma in our early introduction arrived when he came up to the flat to let me know he was leaving, but not before he offered me his turntable to play the few records I owned. I accepted his offer, and then when he left, I cried inconsolably, without understanding why. Maybe it was because he was just so kind.

The Meaning of Chet

Eight in Hebrew is the number of "new beginnings." It is the number for the Hebrew letter *Chet* and means "a fence" or an "inner room." In our daily lives, God places His protective fence around us, hedging out damaging thoughts, actions, plans, and even unhealthy relationships if we allow Him to. Think of this hedge or fence as the boundaries of His instructions, keeping us protected from danger in the same way that the laws of a country are created to protect its citizens and set standards.

For example, in certain countries, wearing a seatbelt is the law to protect in the event of an accident. Consumer laws protect against buying bad products and give people the right to return items. God's laws are the same, providing both protection and grounds to enforce our rights in difficult circumstances. We do this when we pray and act on what we have read. Now Father had given me the mindset to push through change in my life, and just like the Woman, I was able to "throw [myself] into my work."

~

Door 3, Partridge Close

A concealed entrance of a narrow residential road led to the unfurnished, small two-bedroom house within a quiet Chinese community. An overgrown hedge filled the short path leading up to number 3, a brown, wooden front door with latticed pane windows. It was ideal. Sam needed space to play as we had outgrown the second-floor flat where we had lived for three years. The kitchen stood immediately to the left of the hallway, with the main living area straight ahead and a door that led directly onto a large, almost perfectly square but otherwise nondescript garden. With a few rose bushes, the garden seemed suitable for a retirement home; besides the small brown shed standing at the bottom, it had no story to tell.

I had managed to raise the deposit with the help of a work colleague who offered to stand as a guarantor. I will always be grateful to Rita, the accounts office manager I met during my time at the housing association. From the first moment we met, we connected. Rita and I shared the same faith and were raising young boys alone, except that Rita's husband was working abroad. Our similar situations offered a lot to share, and we valued the times we took during lunch to chat and pray, occasionally meeting at weekends.

As the years passed, our lives separated. Yet again, I had seen how Father brings women together, not by chance, but purposely to help and support each other. Sometimes our journeys pass through each other's lives and connect only to make a valuable deposit before moving on. Years later, Rita and I met over lunch and chatted for hours. Neither of us knew it would be the last time we would meet.

College

My parents bought a rug for the front room and a microwave, the first two household items I was to own since the end of my marriage. They even gifted me a remarkable sofa that became the centrepiece of my living room. But let me tell you, this was no ordinary sofa. It had a unique personality of its own. After just an hour of someone sitting on it, it would slowly slide down to reveal its hidden secret—it was actually a sofa bed! You can imagine the surprise when they were left reclining on the floor! Sam and I were the custodians of this little "trick," and we absolutely loved it.

I had accomplished my goal for the prospective year: to have a home for Sam with more space, a garden to play in and a quiet environment to study. That year was the first of five on my journey to becoming a speech and language therapist, and this would be the year I would commit to studying and raising my son with Father's fence to protect us. That summer, my son made many friends in the small neighbourhood and spent evenings riding his bike with the local children until the autumn nights drew in the cold season. That winter became the toughest I had ever known, mentally, physically, and financially, but not spiritually, because I knew that Abba Father was looking after us despite the struggle, and I sensed my character was being further developed.

A single parent and now a mature student, I was entitled to claim a subsidy on the rent, but since moving into the property, the rules had changed, and the council had significantly reduced its financial assistance. As a result, money was very short, and after paying the rent, we were left with just enough to buy basic groceries, travel to college, meet Sam's needs, and pay utilities while his father paid his school fees. This was as much as the finances allowed. To be disciplined with this non-negotiable budget, I bought the same food items every week and did not deviate.

I learned to manage the heating bill by regulating the timer to turn off during the day and come on again in the evening when Sam was back from school until his bedtime. On the non-college days, I worked from home, completing assignments or studying for exams. I would sit in my bedroom working until the timer switched off the heating, after which I would continue under layers of jumpers, watching the windows slowly steam up from my body heat mixing with the cold winter air on the panes.

This situation felt like one of the many fairy stories I had read as a child. Mentally I was prepared as I knew this challenging time of adjustments to accommodate my full-time studies would not last, and the goal of getting a degree and a profession provided much-needed motivation. The tough days were fuelled with vision along with the strength and support of three mature female students I met on the Access course who were also driven to change the direction of their lives. We became pillars for each other by providing support through joint study times, evening calls to discuss research and assignments, and most importantly, sharing lunches, chat, and laughter at the city-based college canteen.

My first lecture took place in a small room overlooking a busy side street filled with shops and offices. A small group of students sat in a semi-circle, listening intently to the psychology lecturer passionately explain socio-economic deprivation and its effects on a community. A tall olive-skinned Middle Eastern man of average height, slight build, and noticeably thick black wavy hair skilfully drew us into the world of political economy. Midway through his discussion, he would casually toss the issue of racism in education into the mix, explaining his belief that his foreign surname was being used as a filter to block interviews at the top universities where he had applied for countless lecturing positions.

I had lived in the vacuum of my life for so long, with little time to consider issues affecting the broader world around me. But this tutor raised awareness of covert racism, setting my mind on exploring areas I had never before considered. And so, there I sat on a quiet weekday afternoon in autumn, listening and engaging in discussions that reached far beyond my everyday interests. What a difference compared to a few months earlier when I was in a busy office, wedged between reconciling purchase invoices and listening to women talk about their hormone replacement treatment (HRT) tablets. Not to say that I didn't find the subject interesting, but at thirty-one, there were other conversations I wanted to have.

One night, after my first day in the office, I fell asleep to the sound of a thudding keyboard playing repeatedly in my head. I had spent many months wondering where my future was heading until late one afternoon, while scanning the local paper at my desk, my eyes were drawn to an advert encouraging mature students to study at university. I knew then my time at the housing association was soon to end.

Such a contrast from that time to sitting in a small classroom in the west of central London, discussing various topics and having my concepts challenged with new information. I got the impression the lecturer felt he was losing sight of being able to teach at a higher-level institution, as his comments were sometimes injected with cynicism about a system stacked against minorities. Until then, I hadn't realised how frustrated I had felt about the direction my life was taking, but not because of a seemingly unfairly weighted system.

The months were shaping up to form one of the most challenging years in my life, mentally and emotionally, and the new journey was about to challenge my determination for success. With the help of family and the women in the college study group, I followed the Woman in 31 by throwing myself into my work. It was a long, lonely year. No visitors came except for my parents and my middle sister, Georgia, when we had dinner together on New Year's Eve. I guess it was a self-imposed isolation, but determined to get the qualification I needed to study at university, I embraced the time and focused my efforts on raising my son while digging the foundation for a new career. My efforts were for him and me.

Ungoze

I realise that people we meet and events in our lives aren't random; there will always be an exchange of some sort, whether we are giving, receiving, or both. I believe God sends people into our lives at the right moments. One such instance was my introduction to an elegant, beautiful West African woman walking arm-in-arm with her fiancé along an East London Underground platform. Her fiancé was a mutual acquaintance of my first husband and me, and he introduced me to Ungoze. Her makeup was impeccably applied, like that of an artist's paintbrush on a canvas, and her hair was styled in a manner that rarely changed and became a consistently recognisable feature of her appearance. She had a beautiful wide smile and soft brown eyes, and her face emanated warmth and gentleness. Later that year, my husband and I attended their wedding with our son two months away from being born.

Six years later, circumstances brought Ungoze and I together, and my place at number 3 Partridge Close was a short five-minute walk from where she lived. Sadly, with our marriages broken, we were alone and caring for young children. Ungoze and I, however, spent many happy times together, eating, listening, advising and consoling each other through difficult times while Sam and her sons played together for hours.

Our friendship was about supporting each other, both practically and spiritually, and gave us hope. Ungoze was a strong believer in Yeshua (Jesus) and passionate about her faith, and during our times together, we would pray for each other and listen to what Father was saying to us. I couldn't have asked for a better friend. Then just as gently as she came into my life, our paths separated.

Years later I spotted her standing at a bus stop. We hugged and talked excitedly, trying to cram as many words about our lives into the brief moments we had. Ungoze was happily remarried, and her boys all grown up. Her face was still a portrait of graciousness, calm, and beauty. We hugged again as we remembered those years now far behind us and grateful for Father's care ever present in our lives. The red London bus pulled up at the stop, and we said our goodbyes without exchanging numbers. Our moments had played out, and the friendship had fulfilled its purpose.

Boxes

A year after moving into the property, our time at number 3 ended abruptly with a move out of the property on the exact date we moved in. Yet again, it appeared that God had planned ahead. For at least three months, large cardboard boxes packed with non-essential household items filled the narrow passageway. Unexpectantly, the landlord had given notice that she was planning to return to her property at number 3. The council, on the other hand, would not re-house us, stating that since I had chosen to rent in the private sector, we were no longer eligible. There was one condition, though: I had to wait for an eviction letter, followed by bailiffs, after which I would be categorised as homeless and eligible for re-housing in temporary accommodation. With no options other than having to reluctantly choose this depressing and embarrassing route, I packed up most of our belongings and waited for the grim outcome.

Daily, I would look at the boxes as I walked by or from the living room while trusting that Father, the Aleph and Strong Leader of my life, would fence my mind against worry and take care of us. The boxes soon became a visual reminder of God's faithfulness to us. So, I waited with the boxes and trusted God for a new beginning. Then the time came to make a decision, which I later realised was God's heart. This action supported the Bible verse that says the steps of a good man [or woman] are ordered by the Lord; and He delights in his [or her] way (Psalms 37:23 KJV).

By taking control of that looming day and deciding to leave, my father had mentioned the wait for council re-housing was an additional stress I didn't need. So he and my mother offered the money for a deposit on another place. Although I was reluctant to accept, I realised this gift was from God. Throughout this ordeal, I had been praying for guidance as I had felt uncomfortable about taking the council's advice with a young child. The decision was made, and we moved again. With the first year now completed and university on the horizon, I opened my front door for the first time to someone, who was about to stand on the periphery of my life. I welcomed his friendship slowly and cautiously from a distance of observation.

Records

On a warm July evening, I opened the door at number 3 to Andrew, my neighbour from number 39. He was about to be placed on the periphery of my life as I cautiously observed him from a distance. He stood looking down at me again, with his forever-kind and warm smile, just as the first time but with no drama of a water leakage!

He carried a yellow and black bag on his shoulder, which I later found out he called "the record bag," where he carried a selection of vinyl. His passion and his heart, as I later found out, lay in that bag within the sleeves of the soulful melodies of the records he had carefully chosen to share with me.

He came into my home amongst the boxes, and we sat in the front room eating, chatting, and playing music. Little did he know how much I appreciated his music, having spent my teenage years with young musicians who introduced Georgia and me to a wealth of classics within that genre. That summer evening, the vibrant and happy sounds filled every corner of my home and brought the first of many special moments with Andrew. After the needle of the turntable he had given me almost two years earlier traced the last sounds on the final record, he swung the yellow and black bag over his shoulder and strolled into the warm night to catch the evening bus home.

That year, Father fenced us in and kept worry far away from my mind, which like the Woman in 31, allowed me the privilege of raising a little boy while completing the first year of higher education, managing a small budget, and moving to another new home. Samuel enjoyed many happy moments at number 3, enjoying more space, the most important reason for the move, and many happy moments playing with the local neighbourhood children during the summer months. God's fence in our life eclipsed the one I first noticed, the light brown one, in the nondescript garden with its corner shed.

Chapter 9

Embracing and Accepting Closure

TET
She sees that her business affairs go well;
her lamp stays lit at night.

Number 13 Hubert— the name of the road had a lovely sound, Hubert. Once vocalised, its warm tones carried invitation, comfort, warmth, and friendship; it assured me we would be safe. I liked the name. Number 13 became the incubator of plans and major decisions that affected my future. At the early mid-point of my life, number 13 welcomed my thirties, and like the Woman in 31, my "lamp" was God's words directing my decisions and right choices.

I made many mistakes, but they became perfect opportunities to learn how to apply his Words to my life, and Father worked everything out for good, just like He had promised in Romans 8:28. Thirteen Hubert became a balance between surging happy feelings and desperately crushing times. Yet God was there to help me work through my emotions, behaviour, and character insufficiencies on those days when I hadn't the faintest idea of what I needed. I didn't get all the answers I wanted, but I learned to trust and be patient. Most of all, He brought closure to certain matters.

My mother and I walked the short distance from her home to the estate agents, where we picked up the keys to door number 13. The property sat nestled in a small residential street within a row of terraced houses. The first detail I noticed was the black and white triangle tiles paving the ground leading up to a light brown wooden front door with stained-glass triangle windows. My parents stood behind me, watching me tentatively turn the key in the door. Because this had now become the familiar routine I had experienced many times, the usual high expectations of the contents behind the door had long disappeared. This time, though, I wasn't disappointed.

The door opened to a hallway flooded with light, the smell of new carpet, and the shine of newly polished dark wood floors. The stairs led to two bedrooms, but not before passing a coloured lattice window, shaping the glass into tiny geometric shapes. I stopped and looked through the window onto a well-kept, modestly sized garden, complete with a wooden arch. The house was perfect, and as I stepped into the hallway, I knew I could study there, and Sam and I would be happy. Later that morning, I listened to my father's prayer as we stood in the main room holding hands while he prayed into our future. The words he spoke were comforting and, as I soon discovered, accurately predictive of future events.

∾

The Meaning of Tet

Tet, the ninth letter of the Hebrew alphabet, amongst other meanings, represents the letter of decision and is linked to the eighteenth verse of Proverbs 31. When faced with choices, we can decide to progress or stagnate, so how do we know which decision to make?

The Bible proverbs emphasise the importance of identifying people who can give good advice. One verse reads, "Plans go wrong for lack of advice; many advisers bring success." (Proverbs 15:22). This statement indicates the key to success is actively searching for the right advice from more than one person. The proverbs have a lot to say about making decisions, taking advice, planning and having the right people in our lives.

Linked with the number nine, the Hebrew letter Tet means "judgement," "finality," and "conclusion." Jesus died at the ninth hour, bringing finality and closure to that part of His work before He, having followed His Father's will, defeated death and came back to life. Summarising the number and meaning of Tet, it appears that one event must close before another opens, and this part of my life was about embracing and accepting closure.

The remaining summer weeks before we moved into number 13 Hubert were filled with unpacking the boxes that had become a hallway fixture at number 3. It felt good to know we were going to be settled for some time, which turned out to be eight years—new beginnings. And like the number nine for Tet, with the advice I had taken, the decision I made to take control of the situation and settle us before the autumn prepared me to close one chapter in my life and open another. Reflecting on this time, I can see God's hands in every detail. Living at number 1 3 gave us the time we needed, long enough for Sam to enjoy his primary school years and for me to earn my university degree, start a professional career, and much more.

University: "Her Lamp Stays Lit at Night"

October arrived in time for the start of a four-year degree in speech and language therapy at City University London. Time is never late. It all felt surreal as I looked up at the tall, rustic Victorian brick building of the main campus in the middle of Northampton Square, London. It would take at least two and half years into the degree to develop the self-confidence to believe I could achieve this level of education; I had periods of doubt that God challenged by using unavoidable situations. The first in my family to go to university, I had no one to advise on the process, but I had much support from family and friends. My parents and siblings, in many different ways, were the support I needed during those four years.

My sister Georgia worked as an employment advisor during that time and was the one to direct me to a career in speech and language therapy. It was a cold February morning as we sat in the warm kitchen of her top-floor apartment with panoramic views of the city where you could see for miles. Resting on the kitchen worktop, I watched as Georgia, with her long jet-black hair tied in a tousled bun just above her neck, opened the fridge and reached for the ingredients to prepare the evening meal we were to share with her baby daughter.

"I'm thinking of changing careers—perhaps social work?" I started.

"Why social work?" She turned to look at me with her dark brown, enquiring eyes.

"Well, I'd like to work with the public in a supportive way."

It was a vague answer, as my professional direction was influenced by a social worker I had met during a career event. We had a short conversation, and on hearing my interest in speech therapy, her words, as a fellow black woman, were swift to dissuade and redirect me to join the majority in social work.

My sister left the kitchen, returning with her trusted careers handbook to flip through the pages to the caring professions.

What about speech therapy? She looked up at me with the satisfied look you see on the face of a jubilant board game winner.

"How could you have guessed?" I remember saying, or something along those lines. That weekday evening discussion brought the confirmation!

I was on a high during the first year, and I knew it would be a pivotal point in my life, a special year, and one I would never forget. It proved amongst many, one of the happiest and most fulfilling years in my life, where everything financial and emotional lined up to form an exciting progression of bright days. During Freshers week, I met with a few of the girls I had studied with during the Access Course as well as other students of the same age and younger who were starting the degree. I was aware God had helped me turn a corner and was continuing to see the plans I made unravel.

We excitedly explored the university campus, familiarising ourselves with the library, which was spread across several floors. We discovered the annexes where lectures would take place, the canteen, student rooms, and the small bar where we would sometimes meet. I fell in love with the location of the university, which straddled campuses between Georgian properties and retail shops in the leafy Farringdon area. At the end of long lectures, there was always the option for a short, quiet stroll to the Barbican or Farringdon Station or a brisk walk through bustling Islington to Angel Station, but not before being enticed by the aromas of freshly ground coffee and tempted by the mouthwatering display of fresh pastries arranged in the local shops' windows along the way.

Friends

The friendship between Andrew and I was growing, and there were times I sensed the relationship had the potential to progress, but the thought made me uncomfortable. He seemed genuinely caring, and everything he did for me felt effortless, not like he was trying to impress. But only time would tell if this was truly who he was. He was considerate concerning the small, mundane things in my life, like one afternoon when he came over to the house with a light bulb and a bottle of milk I needed but hadn't the time or forgot to buy. I hadn't asked for help, so I was amazed at his thoughtfulness, but for reasons I chose to ignore, I was determined to keep some distance. I guess I still hadn't come to terms with the finality of my marriage, even though by now, we had been divorced for over a year. I still hadn't reached closure for that troubled time in my life; I remained wounded and broken, but God remained the constant Light I needed in my life.

Papers

I remember vividly the dull autumn morning when the final divorce papers arrived; still God's Light shone brighter. I opened the envelope and briefly skimmed over the sad, fateful, and conclusive keywords that closed the doors on the first part of my life. That morning, I drove my son to the small, private church school Georgia had recommended as her daughter was attending. We met outside the gates, and I was glad she was there to speak with that morning. I don't remember whether she had planned to take the day off work, but I didn't go to the university, and she drove me straight to Oxford Street in central London and bought me a pair of shoes! That was just like Georgia, using shopping as remedial therapy.

I will never forget the headache I experienced that morning. I could feel a tension in the back of my head stiffening with every bump in the road. The tree-lined Westminster Street leading up to the famous London clocktower, Big Ben, had lost its allure as my eyes strained to manage increasing pain rather than capture the iconic stretch of road separated by the River Thames.

I sat still and quiet in an attempt to allow my body a few minutes to recover, but the blood vessels in my head began to throb and pulsate, pushing away any opportunity to escape the coming pain. It was too much. I succumbed and lay down on the back seat to ease the pressure of both the pain and the end of my marriage. I couldn't believe it was over, but a new, exciting beginning lay ahead.

Letting Go

The months ahead didn't make the end of my marriage any easier. I maintained a growing friendship with Andrew, whom I continued to keep at a distance as I mourned the loss of my marriage, or so I believed. In reality, I couldn't handle the raw emotion of rejection. Occasionally, I would take notice of this amazing man who remained undaunted by my emotional distance, but I quickly pushed away the thought; I didn't want to think about the possibility of a future with Andrew.

There are moments in your life when certain songs become significant, and music played an important part in my life. During my first university year, the retrospective lyrics about a broken relationship by the artist Lauryn Hill played constantly in my head.

It could all be so simple,

But you'd rather make it hard;

Loving you is like a battle,

And we both end up with scars.[1]

Blackheath

Then one day in Blackheath in South London, Georgia and I were walking across the grassy heath, and I couldn't stop crying. She did her best to console me, but then something incredible happened—God spoke. He moved my thoughts aside and made His voice unmistakably clear and distinct.

---

1. *The Miseducation of Lauryn Hill,* vinyl recording (Ruffhouse: Columbia, 1998).

"Women try hard to fix their men and end up getting hurt in the process." He continued, "You need to wait and let Me do the fixing."

With this wisdom imparted, everything suddenly became clear, and things changed. I changed. And even though I understood that only God could "fix" lives, I also knew it was time to let go. It was too late for us. I had been determined, doing as much as I could to mend the relationship, and now it was time for me to move on and take back my life and dignity. It was time to realise my worth and what was acceptable and what was not. And like Tet, meaning "finality" and "decision," that time had arrived.

Something made me smile that afternoon. With eyes red and swollen from crying and not expecting to see anyone, Georgia and I drove to my younger sister Leah's house to find she had friends over. You'll never believe who one of them was. It was Andrew. He looked at me, smiled, and commented positively on my hair, proving God certainly has a sense of humour and timing!

Friendship Journeys

As with any university degree, the challenges it presented were immense. Some of these challenges were to my confidence, ability, consistency, and skill at refining my thinking. As I mentioned earlier, there were often times I thought I would never get my degree, but family, friends, and now Andrew kept pushing me forward. The long nights and early mornings of study and reading God's words kept the "lamp" bright during those dark moments. Over time, I became more stable emotionally and watched myself develop in confidence. Then, almost three years into my four-year degree, friendship having progressed to love, Andrew asked me to marry him. I said yes! But let me tell you how it happened.

Recurring Words

Our friendship had continued to grow. It was the simple things we enjoyed that featured as most important in our relationship: going for drives with long discussions, eating takeaways in the car while listening to our favourite music, spending time with family and friends and being encouraged by the words we heard in our church, and above all, sharing our faith through debate, discussion, reading, and praying together when we got a chance. If I can describe it that way, our faith became the third dimension and gave insight into each other's lives.

All along, I continued asking God whether Andrew would be the man to share my life. I wanted God to confirm through the small things because that's what mattered. I don't remember when my feelings changed from friendship to love, but it was reciprocal. From the time he briefly held my hands at his mother's funeral for comfort and reassurance, I knew he was special. Although it was very early in our relationship, I held his hands back, which for me was a mix of wanting to support a friend at such a sad time in his life and a silent affirmation of his early affection.

The Blue Velvet Box

The slow, careful revealing of a small velvet box set the stage for Andrew's proposal. He opened it tentatively as if his very heart was inside. There, fixed in thick pale cream satin, was a large sapphire circled by small diamonds. I immediately remembered God's words to me that anxious afternoon back in my parents' home when my mother had read the words from the prophet Isaiah: "I will rebuild you on a mountain of sapphires." I had never spoken to Andrew about this, so he had no idea of the Words spoken into my life. That made the engagement ring even more meaningful and symbolic of the rebuilding Father had already started and the promise He had made all those years ago. Despite the time that may have passed, God's promises are always present and waiting to be seen in your life. Don't give up.

Coming to an End

Five years of academic study were about to come to an end, and Samuel was nearing his final year in primary school and preparing for secondary education. This was not only a critical time of great transition for us but also a time to make another decision in my life that would affect Sam and now Andrew.

While facing the last stage of the four-year degree, completing a dissertation, and being stressed, I was also thinking about the future. I was desperate to settle and live somewhere permanent. Most of all, I wanted stability for Sam. Money was tight, and I was looking for the right school for Sam. I was also worried I wouldn't complete my research project on time as I lost all the data I had accumulated over the summer months due to problems with the university software I was using. Feeling responsible, my university lecturer gave me the option of extending the project through the summer and graduating in autumn. But I was tired and desperate to complete it in time and graduate with my peers. I wasn't thinking straight or rationally, and most of all, I was ignoring God's gentle directions to make the right decision. Like the Woman in 31, I wanted my business affairs to go well, but I asked Father to step back and let me take charge. The worry I stubbornly held resulted in a decision that caused a mess for everyone.

Decisions

Tet is about finality and making decisions, and this was one decision I was prepared to make alone. Having reached the end of the degree, I was looking towards the future and how we would move forward. After a series of setbacks, Andrew was rebuilding his life, and although fully committed to getting married, things were moving slowly, and I became anxious and impatient. At the same time, I later realised my ex-husband was reflecting on our past relationship.

My ex-husband and I spoke; then he spoke, and I listened and slowly began entertaining the idea of us starting a new life together. In a surreal moment of trying to recapture the past to create a future, I buried the love I had for Andrew and the commitment we had made and listened to empty dreams, which neither I nor my ex-husband could realise. We should have forgiven each other and forgotten the past, but the promise of a new life together, a home, and the thought of Sam having his dad was enough for me to consider making a decision that would lead to a place where I would find myself alone, dealing with parts of my life I had buried during those years of study. The idea of entertaining a time now past was brief and did not move beyond the boundaries of a few discussions and two evening meals in his busy cafe punctuated with interruptions from staff. This was all too familiar with a past I had left behind. But that was enough. I made the wrong decision, which God used to get me to face myself alone, ask the hard questions, and find answers that only time and a counsellor could achieve.

On that awful afternoon when I called Andrew and ended our engagement, I handed back the sparkling sapphire—the promise—which I would never see again. I don't know when the realisation hit my ex-husband and me, but after a few short weeks of discussion, we, or certainly I, recognised that the decision was wrong. I was devastated! My emotions were raw, and at that point I realised I had lost Andrew, the man who had given me the will to start again. I lost everything God had given us to build a relationship based on trust, friendship, love, and a commitment to share our lives. I had lost the blue gemstone in Andrew, my sapphire, which I couldn't accept as mine. My head was a mess, but more importantly, I felt that I had damaged the man who had stood beside and supported me during the hardships of my university years. Our friendship and relationship were gone. The one area of our lives we hadn't shared, however, was a sexual relationship due to our faith.

A few weeks later, my ex-husband and I arranged to meet, and as the evening wore on, it became increasingly obvious to me that I had made the wrong decision. It later emerged that his focus on starting our lives again was compromised. Too much had passed, and our lives had diverged, we had changed, and the reality was that we were now divorced.

I left our meeting and drove the long journey back to East London with thoughts crashing around in my head. I was an emotional wreck! I drove my father's car, which I had borrowed, back to my parents' home and posted the keys through the letter box. It was now around 1:30 in the morning, and I decided to take the night bus, then a short walk to my home. My head was filled with the consequences of the crazy decision I'd made. I got off the bus a few stops early to give myself time to think, and then it started to rain. It was that dark night road I was walking down when the kind stranger asked me if I was okay. The futility of my foolish decision clung to me more than my rain-soaked clothing. I had lost nearly everything that mattered and was faced with a solitary version of myself and months of empty space ahead. I finally got home, turned the key in the lock, and then closed the door on messed up relationships to face a woman who couldn't heal.

Summer

Father spent the rest of the summer with me, and there was nowhere to hide this time. My degree was finished, and I didn't start work until the early autumn. My days were spent alone, and I had time to think. It was clear I was still in love with Andrew, but I had conveniently buried those emotions to "do the right thing" and heal the rejection, which for years I carried but refused to admit. The decision was wrong; *my* decision was wrong, but it was too late, and that was clear. So at age thirty-six, I found myself alone again, but God had brought the situation to its conclusion.

Chapter 10

Finding Wholeness

YOD
She puts her hands to the staff with the flax
her fingers hold the spinning rod.

That summer was one of the toughest emotionally, even more so than previous experiences. Exposing what was deeply buried in my life, my feelings became part of the ongoing healing process God was doing, and despite the sometimes lonely and painful days, I began to mend.

During that time, I heard of a woman who, having gone through a painful ending of an abusive relationship, decided to repaint her entire home as a gesture symbolic of healing her memories, and it worked. As I gazed at the tired-looking walls in my house, I couldn't help but relate to their lacklustre state. Since I had finished my degree and was simply waiting for the results, I thought it was the perfect time to give the walls a fresh new look by giving them a coat of white and ivory paint. My decision to repaint was a mixture of trying out the woman's approach and taking the challenge of decorating the walls myself as an opportunity to fill the time while Samuel was away on holiday in New York. It was an attempt to ease the pain of my breakup and the subsequent loneliness.

I purchased tubs of paint, brushes, masking tape, and paper to cover the carpet and began the attempt to paint over my pain. However, God had another plan, and this time He wasn't going to allow me to decorate over my life as I had previously. So I painted, reflected, prayed, painted, cried, and painted while I healed and prayed until, finally, the large surface area started to look clean and bright. I was happy with it.

The weeks went by, and I was missing Andrew. I was beginning to realise the extent of what I had thrown away and how much I loved him. The summer days were lonely, and the evenings were long. I had been used to spending them with Andrew, doing things of little importance or, at the other end, being serious and planning for the future, but whatever we chose, we always enjoyed our time together—a sharp contrast to the days I now experienced in a house empty and silent because he should have been there. I tried to fill the time in whatever way I knew, but the void remained.

~

The Meaning of Yod

"You made me; you created me. Now give me the sense to follow your commands."

—Psalms 119:73

The number for the Hebrew letter "Yod" is ten, which signifies "fullness," filled entirely to capacity with God's Words. It is linked to the nineteenth verse in Proverbs 31. There are many examples showing the significance of the number ten, but one of the most important references is found in Exodus, where God gave the Hebrews the Ten Commandments, also known as the "Ten Words."

The Ten Words were given to establish and bring order to a newly forming community. They were complete, bringing divine order and establishing the everyday lives of God's people. The symbol for Yod looks like an arm reaching up towards heaven. Like its pictorial representation, it means "arm," "hand," and "the offer of friendship or help." It can also mean "actions," "work," and "strength."

An Ancient Work Tool

The image presented is one of the Woman at work. When it says, "she puts her hands to the staff with the flax," I interpret the verse to mean, "she puts God's words to work by applying them in real-time to her life." We won't see the results of God's promises unless we apply them to daily life. When we read then apply, this action can be defined as trust or faith. We hear, we move, and God provides what we need. It's the everyday experiences that test the Word, and then we see the Father's ability to give us His hands of strength to hold, support, guide, and protect.

The verse talks about the Woman working with an ancient piece of equipment called a spinning rod or wheel. Descriptions of this device present strong images of hard work with low pay and a very basic existence; however, further investigation shows that this was not the case.

The book of Exodus describes the different types of work needed to build a space where God could meet with His people. This building was going to be amazing, but God explained He didn't need a place to be worshipped. Still, He accepted David's offer, but the building would be accomplished by his son, Solomon. When the construction started, everyone needed to be on board, men and women. The women who came forward to contribute were probably at the top of their professions, highly skilled, and they brought the most expensive gifts made from the highest quality materials of their time. This tells us that when we bring God's wisdom (His approach) into our work, we succeed every time, despite the odds. In fact, He works well with "odds." The writer talks about the Woman's hands and the work she is about to do. The ten fingers on our hands represent the strength we have to achieve anything we put our minds to when we apply God's Words to every situation, no matter how difficult. The promise in the book of Isaiah chapter 43, verse 2 (CJB), says:

> **"When you pass through water, I will be with you; when you pass through rivers, they will not overwhelm you; when you walk through fire, you will not be scorched —the flame will not burn you."**

~

Write Him a Letter

In a last panicked attempt to mend the relationship with Andrew, I decided to write a letter to explain myself clearly. That evening I posted my thoughts through his letterbox and walked away, hoping it would bring the outcome I desperately wanted, which was having my friend and the man I loved back in my life. He called a few days later, and we agreed to meet for lunch.

It had been a few months since the breakup, and I was optimistic. After all, Andrew was caring and forgiving, and I had a long story to tell. I hoped the two combined would be enough. We met, and my feelings confirmed that I still loved him. I just wanted him to hold my hands with his gentle but firm grip, walking quietly together, saying nothing. He looked at me with his kind face and smiled as I tried to read his intentions, but the initial gesture was far removed from what I had imagined would follow. His facial expression, I soon understood, was a sanitising non-verbal message conveying, "I've read the letter and thank you for offering an explanation!" It was not what I had hoped for.

I realised then I had misjudged his feelings and run ahead of God's timing again. He was angry and hurt. We spent the short time we had arguing, and the afternoon drained away with him walking towards the Underground, leaving me standing in the middle of Canary Wharf, London's Financial District. In happier days it had been a place we enjoyed meeting to drink coffee and plan our futures amidst the busy city workers and the towering glass office tower blocks.

As I stood in the square watching him disappear into the crowd, the buildings appeared to elevate from the ground, closing in around me, and the sunlight bouncing off the glass panes turned against me like daggers to further inflict pain. Despite the warm sunny afternoon and the many trees and hedges strategically planted to soften the sharp aesthetics of a working environment, this time the area looked sterile and harsh. The journey home was the longest I could have imagined. I sat in the bus, watching people and buildings drift past as I tried to hold back tears.

The long summer days continued with me running to the solace of prayer, and as the silence grew louder between Andrew and me, I realised the relationship may have ended. I needed to prepare to let go.

When summer ended, I was due to start my professional career as a speech and language therapist, feeling both excited and anxious at the same time. My routine was about to change again, and after a long battle with my local education services to secure the right secondary school for Sam, we were both just about ready to embrace the change, but not before God clearly spoke to me. I couldn't understand why it appeared other women could move on after relationships, but not me. Why was I still stuck and needing more time? I spent a lot of time reviewing my life and concluded that I needed time to be completely alone. I prayed and read scriptures until, one afternoon, I was clear about what needed to happen next.

The Burying Ritual

God helped me understand some people didn't "move on" but became, as I would describe, experienced at "burying the bones" of past relationships. Father explained he didn't want me to brush over endings in that way. Instead, with His support, I had to face them. To be able to experience the completeness of loving and being loved, there should be no "graves" with the "headstones" of past relationships in my life. I had to allow Father to heal me as I forgave my ex-husband and myself.

As I pondered this new understanding, I realised that I had followed what I now call the "burying ritual." It became the reason I was unable to move on, continually returning to that painful place. I had perfected this behaviour, which prevented me from fully committing to Andrew and the reason behind our stilted relationship, despite the fact I had committed to sharing a future with a man who had clearly loved me. I just couldn't see it. I resolved that if we were to meet again, there would have to be no graves.

Only God could heal me, slowly, over time, and it began by admitting the mistakes I had made and receiving His love, forgiveness, and healing. Although I cried a lot over those months, I knew the tears were allowing the healing process to begin. In particular, as I remembered every painful event, word, and action, God reassured me He was healing the memories on the days and hours they occurred. My past was no longer wrapped in pain but unravelling with forgiveness and healing.

In the weeks after our meeting, my attempts to call were met with short, cold responses, often punctuated with his silence, leaving me feeling awkward, wishing I hadn't called. So I stopped. As the months passed, I experienced a sense of satisfaction that wasn't dependent on feelings; it was God's joy. At the same time, I started my new career. Then slowly the phone conversations increased like the reviving of a beating heart rate after injury. It was evident that God was at work in Andrew's life. Although I welcomed the conversation, I didn't anticipate anything further. During that time we did not meet. There was no social media then, so it was basic: text, call, or leave a voicemail. However, each time we spoke, communication was clearer, and we were able to express our thoughts without arguing.

Completeness

Then one late autumn afternoon, we agreed on a time to meet. It was now mid-September, and the summer was ending with heavy, warm rain. Andrew stood in the kitchen as I cooked, and we talked. I will never forget what happened next. As I turned around to face him in conversation, there he stood with his arms wide open. Without hesitation, I went straight to him, and he hugged me for what seemed like forever. At the risk of seeming overly dramatic, I must describe the rain. It was pouring down, creating a symphony of drum-like beats on the plastic roof sheeting that covered the extension of the kitchen area. As loud as it was, my heart beat louder. This was Father giving me His arms through total healing now with the ability to love and be loved.

This was a "Yod season" in my life, a fulfilling time, and as I allowed God to work in my life, He offered me His hand of strength, which I desperately needed but could not see. God, the Strong Leader of my life, rich and generous, reached down to pick up and mend what no one else could. With His understanding of what was happening, He helped me to identify the darkness in my life as I allowed Him to make the necessary changes. Now I had closure and an opportunity to start again.

Chapter 11

Accepting God's Embrace

KAF
**She reaches out to embrace the poor and
opens her arms to the needy.**

I was blessed and privileged to be the daughter of a loving father; I couldn't have asked for better. The vivid image I have is one I will never forget, so strongly etched in my memory I could touch it. I must have been around five years old. I was at school and feeling very ill. The story my parents told me about the first year of my life was that soon after I was born, I developed what was then known as bronchitis and spent many weeks in the intensive care unit. Following that episode, my health remained unstable, and each winter, the respiratory difficulties returned, leaving me with short, laboured breaths from heavily congested lungs. During these episodes I was confined to bed and missed weeks from school. But despite the discomfort, it was always a special time with my parents wrapping me in warm blankets and giving extra care.

Our family doctor was tall, and whenever he entered the room with one of my parents, I always noticed his large black bag, brown tweed jacket, wavy brown hair and spectacles, over which he would peer down at me as he listened to my wheezing chest through the stethoscope that always hung around his neck. His recommendations became a matter of routine: "plenty of fluids and rest," but not without the penicillin dispensed in dark bottles by the local pharmacist.

The doctor's prescription was followed by my parents' remedy of the orange fizzy drink called Lucozade, which always came in generous wrappings of orange cellophane. The Lucozade, mixed with Ribena, turned into a thick sweet syrup that became the nurturing remedy designed to speed up recovery. The aroma of mint tea always made an appearance to a reluctant little girl, though years later, I would come to love the drink reminiscent of the past.

Over the weeks my breathing became less rattled and laboured, which was a clear sign of my health getting back to normal. That particular afternoon in the nursery school, I remember sitting cross-legged on the wooden floor, waiting patiently for my dad to arrive. The scene of that moment remains strong in my mind. Upon his arrival, he held a brief conversation with the teacher, picked me up, and carried me home. That cold winter's day, as he took his long strides walking briskly through the heavy snow, I bounced gently up and down to match the rhythm and movement of his steps. Dad's hands mirrored God's open, loving hands, carrying me during the most intense moments.

A Road Less Travelled

My father, the youngest of fourteen children, was born to a large, wealthy family. By the time Dad was born, his parents were fairly advanced in age, and as her last son, his mother loved him dearly. My grandfather was a school headmaster and parented his son with the authoritative hands of traditional Victorian values and high expectations. He was yet to realise that this headstrong child nurtured his own ideas about life and was not going to conform to my grandfather's exacting standards. George—my father—would blaze his own trail.

My father told many stories of his childhood, and his detailed storytelling would paint vivid, colourful images in our minds of his days on the beautiful Caribbean Island of Dominica. Despite access to money and privilege, stories from his youthful days supported the kind and unselfish man we knew as our dad. The young man he described was known among his friends as kind and generous, and being brought up in a wealthy family, he lived a lifestyle many young people on the island could only dream of. My Father was liberal, giving away money and clothes as needed to his friends, not to buy friendships, but to meet needs, and because of his character, his friends loved him.

These early characteristics continued to develop through the tough times ahead after leaving the Caribbean in the early sixties for a new life in England, where my mother soon followed. I was the firstborn, making my dad a twenty-year-old young father, with my brother following two years later. Then the children kept coming in one-year intervals until the fifth and last child was born. Raising five children without the support of family was not easy for my parents. Money was tight, but those tough times forged our characters. After working as a delivery driver for many years, my dad made a bold decision to become a full-time pastor for a small congregation, with my mother's complete support. Yet, he never let his new role overshadow his commitment to our family—being the best father he could be was always his top priority.

I am the woman I am today because of his love and leadership in my life. Along with my dear mother, he provided the platform, determination and courage to excel in life as a woman in any area I chose. Growing up with two sisters and two brothers, household responsibilities were equally divided, and my parents showed us how a husband and wife could love and work together. With five young children, Dad took on as much of the housework as Mum. They modelled the importance of working together and sharing responsibilities equally, life skills that have stayed with us to this day. If I can describe it this way, our observation of Dad was that he led from behind, quietly guiding us in a desired direction without us even realising he was leading.

Dad led by example. He would not use a single word to either advise or encourage without us watching him live it. My dad wasn't perfect, but he was willing to recognise his needs and work for change through the sometimes tough life experiences. On the many occasions we met to talk, I would ask him to listen with either his "pastor's hat" or his "Dad hat," depending on the need. That would always make him smile. Deep down, I believe he listened with both, knowing just when a change of hat was needed. I loved him for that, but now I know it was my mother who was my father's strength in ways we will never know.

I had the privilege of growing up with a loving father, yet I know that's not the case for everyone. For some, the years have left many painful emotions, if any can be felt at all. The healing I described in the previous chapter and discussions I have had with women of faith over many years make me confident to say that God is able to heal those years in the most unique and amazing ways because He knows us. He is the Strength who reaches out to embrace us with open hands, carrying an invitation for us to come to Him. He works through the daily routines and turns of everyday life, piece by piece.

The Meaning of Kaf

There's much to say about the significance of this letter and its numerical value because it's about God's special presence filling our lives. The more time you spend with a person, the more you discover and the stronger the relationship becomes; this is no different with God. After Yod, the tenth letter in the Hebrew alphabet, the numbers increase in multiples of ten. *Kaf*, the eleventh letter in the sequential order of the Hebrew alphabet and linked to the twentieth verse, has a number value of twenty. Its pictograph symbolises an "open hand" lifted up to receive.

God's hands are open and ready to "reach down" to bless and rest on the lives He touches, and then there are times when His blessing is given to move us effortlessly into the next stages of our lives. This only comes after we have received His strength and ability, as described in the previous chapter, as God's open hands rest on our lives through His Son, Yeshua. The Kaf phase is about God reaching out to embrace us with open arms and His hand resting on our lives. Then, as Father has reached out and given to us, we are able to reach out to others. This next stage of my life needed God's embrace, strength, and courage for what was to follow.

Change

The summer of 2003 was the catalyst for immense change in our family's lives beyond what we could ever have imagined. It was a brutal hammer blow for all of us and would lead to lots of embracing and tears as we walked into what seemed like an endless five-year dark night. The previous year, Father had shown me a dream that left me uncomfortable and determined not to analyse it further than what it presented that night. But whether I liked it or not, it clearly signalled change, and it would send intermittent flashes in my head for months. I chose to deny it for months. Now looking back, it presented an opportunity to gently prepare me for what God allowed me to see, but I didn't want that type of preparation.

One Saturday morning, my mum gave me a call and said that Dad wanted to meet with the family. As I prepared to go, I felt uneasy, and my stomach started tying itself into knots. For some time, Dad had been suffering from a running cold that hadn't shifted despite having spent a good few weeks in the Caribbean completing his book. We knew he had been to see his local doctor for a check-up that had led to further investigations. I called Andrew, who told me not to worry and that everything would be fine, but my mind was anxious and my body tense.

A few of my siblings had already gathered by the time I arrived at my parents' house. We waited, tentatively exchanging pleasantries while giving each other furtive, searching looks. It was clear we were all thinking the same thing. When the blow came, it was hard, shattering, heavy, leaving us dazed and without answers. With his dedicated wife by his side, the strong yet gentle character of the man we loved delivered the news to his family as gently and bravely as he could, carefully explaining the doctor's findings: the "shadow" on his lung indicated cancer.

It was a surreal moment that left us all stunned. *How? Why? When?* These searching questions collided in my head for the longest time. Dad bravely tried his best to hide his feelings, which he no doubt shared with Mum. He explained the hospital wanted to operate to remove the disease from the lower left lung. I remembered many promises, but one that stayed with me was a verse from the Prophet Isaiah where God promises to be with us when we go through "waters" and "rivers of difficulty."

"When you go through deep waters, I will be with you. When you go through rivers of difficulty, you will not drown. When you walk through the fire of oppression, you will not be burned up; the flames will not consume you."

—Isaiah 43:2

These Words became God's hand to shield my head from the impact of the hammer's crushing blow. For days after the announcement, I cried a lot, and anxiety gripped my stomach before I could even get out of bed in the mornings. Yet, despite what felt like a chaotic mind, God cleared the anxious thoughts and reminded me again and again that He was with me and I could trust Him fully. As a close family, we were each other's strength. We knew our mother was devastated, but her strong faith remained her foundation. We hugged her, Dad hugged her, we hugged Dad, we hugged each other, and God's character quality of comfort in difficult times embraced us. His open hand rested on us.

We prayed much together in the days ahead, wherever we could. But now leading our own lives, we were together yet alone and, at the same time, trying to make sense of a bad dream. We were told the operation was scheduled soon after the diagnosis and would last many hours since they were going to remove his lower left lung. Dad checked into St. Bart's London Hospital where we met with the female registrar who was to perform the operation. Georgia and I were present while Dad was asked a series of questions, in particular, questions to confirm he was aware of the nature of the operation and that he clearly understood which part of his lung was about to be removed. Our mother found this part of the process distressing and chose not to attend the discussion. We understood. And over time, she chose the position needed to support her husband.

Following the pre-operation consultation, with the procedure scheduled for the early morning, we left Dad at the hospital on a warm summer evening. It was now dusk, and the lights from the hospital wards lit up the small cul-de-sac with the sound of the large hospital generators whirring and filling the air. Walking down the hospital steps leading to the street, we strolled along the side road, looking up to the ward that overlooked the enclosed area, not wanting to leave Dad alone. And as we looked, there he stood, waving at us through the window, slightly ajar, making jokes for us and smiling with that gentle face. That was his character, our dad, always giving us hope even though he was at the centre of his storm. We had no idea what lay ahead and that this would be the last time we would see our dad the way we had always known him.

On the morning of the operation, Dad was shown to a single bed positioned at the front of the ward, where he was later met by the anaesthetist. For that brief moment, he looked vulnerable and almost childlike as he sat on the edge of the hospital bed dressed in the flimsy, faded blue operation gown and at the mercy of events to follow. I just wanted to run over and cuddle and protect him, as we all did, but this was our father's road that only he could walk. God reached out to embrace Dad and, like the Woman in 31, opened His arms to "the needy" as He did with us on what became the longest day in our lives.

The waiting room was small, with a few non-matching but comfortable high-back armchairs arranged around the room. Well-chosen pictures hung on the walls, bringing a welcome deviation from the anxious hours of waiting. Sometimes we didn't want to talk but just sit and think. I was grateful for the thoughtfully decorated room that welcomed friends and family. This was the first major challenge our family faced, but strong bonds held us together.

The hospital garden sat peacefully in what appeared to be a courtyard in the middle of the building and could be seen when walking down the stairs to leave the ward. It was attended by the gardener, who took pride in keeping it well-manicured with his lawnmower and clippers to shape the hedges. A church with hundreds of years of history was tucked away, almost hidden by the towering branches of well-established trees accessible by the general public through a short, narrow walkway. We discovered the church, constructed in 1123, was called St. Bartholomew-the-Less. It provided a welcome respite for hospital staff, family and friends to take time out to reflect, meditate, and pray.

It was warm that day, and the waiting room became stuffy, so Georgia and I took the short walk to the church and sat at the back of the place of worship filled with history and the musky smell of burning incense, stained glass windows, and wooden benches which had provided many hours of solace and prayer. We prayed, too, for what seemed like hours, praying for Dad, praying for Mum, praying for ourselves, and trying to make sense of a surreal situation. But God remained the centre of the event. Afterwards, we slipped out of the sombre atmosphere onto the busy streets to get a coffee with the sun's rays dazzling and dancing in front of our eyes, and, for those brief moments, everything seemed as normal as it had always been.

Afterwards

The doctor remarked her patient was the fittest sixty-year-old man she had ever operated on, and the procedure was successful. Four hours later, and now out of the critical period, Dad was moved onto the ward. However, the relief we felt vanished as quickly as it appeared. The moments that followed would be forever soldered on our memories, and each family member held a fragment of the panic of that moment. Our father was connected to a heart and blood monitoring device and tubes to remove excess liquid from building up in his lungs. In an unexplained moment, looking at me, still groggy from surgery, Dad suddenly rolled his eyes to the back of his head and began to struggle to breathe. We shouted for the nurses, and our lives, from that very moment, appeared to descend into the dark unknown. The last moment I remember was Dad's bed being wheeled by the nurses through the short corridor into the high dependency unit (HDU). They say Dad died that late afternoon as the medical staff fought to bring him back.

In the terror of the moment, we were all scattered—a family together yet apart—and the remaining scenes faded into oblivion, except for the memory of my sister Leah and me being led into a side room by the doctor. Another doctor was already sitting, waiting to gently unfold the devastating news that our father was probably not going to survive the night. There wasn't time to disbelieve what God had clearly told the family, and without effort or planning what we were going to say, we both joined in chorus, "That's not what God said!" which was met with blank stares from both doctors. This was yet another moment of Father reaching out with His hands to embrace because, despite the fear and dread of the thoughts of those moments crashing into our minds like waves, each wave of troubling information carried less impact.

That night was long, but Father embraced us, and His presence or anointing, as it is also called, felt strong amongst us. This was the Kaf: His strong yet gentle hand resting on our minds. We walked back to the small waiting room and formed a circle to hold hands and pray and, as we did, I will never forget the kindness from people of other faiths or of no faith, who politely left the room, granting us time to be alone for those brief moments even though we hadn't asked. These are the moments when people support each other with no barriers. It was a compassionate act of kindness as we stood in the waiting room, now dark, lit only by the hallway and the distant yellow lights from the wards across the balcony facing the waiting room.

The Cubicle

Dad survived, and we lived through the moment of a long experience. It was agreed Mum and I would stay overnight, and the rest of the family left to get some rest. We were grateful the

157

hospital offered this free facility that I can only describe as "the cubicle in the basement." It took some time to find the room as we walked numbly through what seemed like a labyrinth of winding tunnels making up the hospital's central nervous system. We were relieved and grateful to find the room that looked like it had been carved out around the enormous pipes pushing water around the hospital. There was only space for two people, and despite the location, the room was welcoming and peaceful. A book lay open for visitors to write messages expressing gratitude and encouraging words to staff as well as family and friends next to discover the room. It was a very long night, and Mum and I were exhausted. Mum was lost in a world with her husband, for which I have no words to write. They remain her own.

We slept out of exhaustion, and every muscle in my body ached from the shock and stress of the day. The night was filled with the humming of the large hospital generators, which filled every area of the basement. As I closed my eyes, I could still hear the high-frequency pips of the life support machine and the sight of nurses frantically pushing Dad's bed on wheels at speed through the corridor into the HDU. The torturous image replayed again and again, in slow motion, until my mind was too tired to watch. I fell asleep in the stifling heat of a summer night in the basement cubicle, listening to Mum's breaths as she slept.

The morning slipped in respectfully and quietly, and I left to buy some breakfast for us. It was a beautiful morning; the sun had not yet risen, and the air remained crisp and untouched by the fumes of the busy traffic. As I looked up, I could see the sun's first rays behind the clouds, but deep down I wanted to see God. I was desperate to tell Him what had just happened, just in case He was unaware. I wanted to share my story with the few people who crossed my path as they walked by in the same or different directions. I wanted to say, "Hi, did you know I nearly lost my dad yesterday?" I imagined their sympathy, "I'm so sorry to hear," followed by a comforting conversation and a hug. The world needed to know, and I wanted to tell it.

As I crossed the beautiful London square, making my way to the Italian café for coffee and toast, I watched the most beautiful car drive slowly around the square and towards the small road ahead. The silver-blue, open-top 1950s vintage car caught my eye. At that moment, it seemed to personify Dad and God assuring me in those brief seconds that everything was going to be okay. Once again, Father reached out His open hands to the needy.

Despite a health setback, the days and months that followed watched a slow yet steady recovery for Dad, and our lives returned to a near normal for a while. He was given all clear as the operation had been successful, and two clear years followed, during which Andrew and I got married. Then in 2006, a second bombshell dropped on our lives. Regular bouts of flu and alarming episodes of illness signalled a later confirmation that the cancer had returned. Our lives turned another sharp corner.

Chapter 12

Leadership in Challenging Times

LAMED
**When it snows, she has no fear for her household
since all of them are doubly clothed.**

Can I Do This?

After many years of practising my profession, I decided to take a role that would challenge, develop, and fine-tune my skills. At first I was unsure whether to accept the position, but I sensed Father was calling me to it; despite initially turning down the opportunity, I was later urged to accept. I believe we grow quickest in uncomfortable positions, as they extend us and erase limiting self-talk by removing the self-imposed ceiling we place on our lives without being aware.

A few weeks into the role, while walking on the grounds of the building, I heard Father say, "You are more than able to fulfil this role!" During moments of doubt, His words came back to re-align momentary insecurities. We are "more than able," like the Woman in 31, because God has "doubly clothed" us, i.e., He has given us double what we need to manage our lives in every area. When we pray, we invite Father into our day as we meet His mind through His Son, Jesus, and His Spirit, who helps us to pray. If not, we run the risk of assuming we can manage our lives alone until we meet the inevitable wall.

The Meaning of Lamed

Lamed, pronounced "Lamb-ed," is the twelfth number of the Hebrew alphabet with a number value of thirty and is linked to the twenty-first verse. It is symbolic of a shepherd's staff and means to "teach" or "share information." Lamed is also thought to mean "preparation for dark days ahead" if we refuse to listen and choose our own way. The metaphor of "snow" in the verse symbolises many things, but in this context it means tough times, which can bring feelings of worry, anxiety, and even fear.

For the first time, I had been asked to temporarily take a position of leadership during my father's post-operative recovery. The commitment proved to be one of the toughest challenges I had experienced. It was pressured and stressful, and it seemed as though there wasn't a day when I wasn't faced with major decisions. I would wake in the morning not only thinking about the day ahead but also reliving the diagnosis, the recent traumatic events in the hospital, and Dad's full recovery. Then the feelings started. I would wake with my stomach fluttering, and this continued for weeks until one morning, Father, through the gentle voice of His Spirit, made me aware that the fluttering feeling was anxiety. I was able to link this back to the time when Dad gave the family news of his illness and then the mornings I would wake with feelings of worry and fear of the future.

Being able to isolate this emotion and the cause was something only God could have shown, and He was already striding ahead of me. This feeling is acknowledged in the New Testament book of Philippians 4:6–7:

> **"Don't worry about anything; instead, pray about everything. Tell God what you need, and thank him for all he has done. Then you will experience God's peace, which exceeds anything we can understand. His peace will guard your hearts and minds as you live in Christ Jesus."**

In the book of Matthew, Jesus acknowledges that all of us worry at times. However, He wants us to understand prayer as a tool to deal with anxiety. Also, in Proverbs it clearly states that worry leads to ill health!

I began to increase time praying and learned to transfer those anxious feelings to God, the Aleph and Strong Leader of my life. During the days that followed, it was God who "doubly clothed" me. In other words, He increased my ability to take on the role for the time I was asked. Today I'm still learning to give my concerns to God through prayer, reminding myself of His Promises and trusting Him to give the support I need daily. This all takes time and practice and developing consistency in response to problems when they come. This action is supported by having God's Lamed, His instructions in our lives.

The writer gives insight into this Woman's approach to challenges. It shows she's not worried or anxious during tough times or pressured by external influences, e.g., economic factors. She seems to approach her interests—home, family, career, in fact anything she sets her mind to—like a business, with planning and purpose. "Double clothing" is symbolic of Father being present in her life, giving her the ability to manage as she trusts Him for this gift. God gives her the instructions, wisdom, and understanding she needs to function. Despite the responsibilities we have or roles we play as women, we are able to fulfil them because Father gives the ability.

Chapter 13

The Darkness of the Womb

MEM
She makes her own quilts
she is clothed in fine linen and purple.

As a child, I sometimes took on a different role during the long summer school holidays. With both of my parents working full-time to take care of five young children, as the eldest—though a mere child myself—it was up to me to "look after" my younger siblings, whom I fondly referred to as "the children." During those long summer days, the garden became the place to explore and play, and when that was done, I'd carefully build houses shaped from cardboard boxes. I would construct three-storey, spacious houses, with rooms for the matchstick people to wander through, maybe cook a meal in the kitchen, take a shower in the intricately made bathroom, then enjoy a nap on the cardboard beds covered in old, coloured cloth for the bedding and the bedframes fixed firmly with glue. I'm sure I made enough for a village.

When Mum took time from work, as a treat she would take me to the "Ideal Home Exhibition" in London's Earl's Court, which I always loved. I'd watch her unwind as she tried out the new gadgets, and afterwards, I'd happily stand next to her in an endless queue waiting to file through the model life-sized homes with perfect interiors. Ironically, I would eventually discover that life wasn't "ideal," and I would meander through endless addresses. But through all those years, Father stood alongside me, close and accessible during my hidden years.

It's hard to admit, but I lived with shame for years. This was the shame of feeling that I'd not achieved the goals I identified in the timeframes I had set. Nothing wrong with that, you might say, and I agree. However, the difficulty remained that I couldn't understand why my life had taken such a turn and I'd not achieved the goal of home ownership within the timeframe I had set. To a degree, society has made home ownership a rite of passage to adulthood and independence and uses it as a barometer of success and wealth. There is, of course, much to say on that perspective, but the thought of not owning a home was enough to make me hide behind this feeling.

I wanted to fit in with other homeowners; I wanted to use the home ownership language—mortgage, kitchen extensions, new bathrooms, rendering walls and patios. I wanted to live in suburbia with a front and back garden like everyone else. I felt I deserved it. Having moved countless times, as I described earlier in the book, then starting again much later in life, there was much to build. Again, there's nothing wrong with that, nothing at all, but for years I just couldn't bring myself to admit to others except close friends that the home I lived in was not my own. It became my shameful secret. I kept quiet and retreated during discussions when the subject of homes came up while silently, inside, I lay in a heap.

Then one night, I had a dream where I heard Father promising me that amongst my other heart desires, I would own a home. I grew excited, but as time went on, I began to wonder if it would ever happen. God's timings seldom match our own, and that's the tough part. But while we wait, He builds our character, and amid all that, He wanted to heal me from shame.

One afternoon, as I sat reading and listening to a speaker talking about emotions from a Christian perspective, I felt the gentle direction of Father moving me to talk to Him about the raw feelings I'd carried for years. And as I began to speak, the feelings surfaced and there it was: shame. I hated it and couldn't bring myself to say the name. Hours seemed to pass that afternoon, but when I finished praying, I felt light—the lightest I had felt for the longest time—and I realised that God had healed and taken away the feeling of shame that I'd carried. Days later, I washed my hair, and as I looked in the mirror, Father gently moved me on to the next transition in my life, and I stopped hiding behind the extensions I had worn for years to cover my own hair.

This was my journey to birth from my own womb, if I can describe it that way, and it was time to allow Father to allow me to give birth to *me*. I had only one request: when Andrew came home to see the new me, I wanted him to affirm it. After his car pulled up outside that evening, I heard his footsteps approaching the door. I stood there, nervous, as he opened the door to see me waiting. I watched as his eyes traced my hair then shifted to my face.

"It's beautiful," he said with a knowing smile.

The warmth of his words wrapped around me like a receiving blanket swaddling a newborn.

The Vision in Your Womb

To carry a vision, a "womb vision" as I call it, is to have a desire and then a plan to work on the steps to get there. It can be years in the making, with the possibility of setbacks. It's what you can see that no one else can, and when shared, people, whether openly or secretly, may not share the belief that you can achieve it. Initially, others may briefly feel the excitement of what you are planning, but as the days, months, or years pass, their support begins to fade, and they may even respond with negative thoughts or words. The Bible gives firm instruction for this saying:

> **"Above everything else, guard your heart; for it is the source of life's consequences."**
>
> **—Proverbs 4:23 CJB**

Our plans, dreams, and visions are tied to our emotions, whether we like it or not. So over a process of time, it's necessary for God to build strength in our character so we can manage the plans when they become real. Our emotions are like waves moving in and out and, if left unchecked, can hinder the process and timing of His plans. For example, days feeling discouraged may affect your ability to work on a project, so time is lost.

It's important to guard your plans, dreams, and visions. Think twice about who you share your plans with because your wide, open heart comes with that conversation, showing the person the highway to the intimacy of your life. You could liken it to inviting a stranger or someone you don't know very well straight into your bedroom. Pray and ask God to show you who to share with, and while you wait, "guard your heart." Then there are days when the vision is clear with detailed planning and action but then seems to fade. This is when God gives clarity and encouragement to push forward.

Push Forward

I remember driving to the supermarket one late afternoon in early spring, and I was feeling low about plans I had made that seemed to have stalled—again. As I drove into the car park, I noticed an advert on a small white van which read, "Don't give up on your dreams." It had a dual meaning. I realised then that God was talking as He does through His written words and in life's everyday occurrences. It wasn't the first time God had spoken to me using advertisements. Of course, we don't look for our environment to speak, but we do look for God to speak through any means He chooses. The message to Mary spoken by the angel made it clear that "with God nothing is impossible."

While You Wait

The womb is core to a woman, whether she has children or not; it is her centre. As part of the reproductive system, it moves through a cycle of change every month in preparation for the body and the woman to create a life. It is also one of the places where hormones are made. Metaphorically, the womb is where we hold our visions, dreams, and plans in a concealed place. Although dark, it is the location for a perfect design and build.

During my review of this manuscript, I realised I had subconsciously moved the focus away from my story to the descriptions of the Woman. It was easier. This part of the book was the hardest to express because I later realised the womb was the birthing place of *me*—my children, my dreams and my long journey—and I had to own this reality. As I was writing this book, I felt I was giving birth to ideas I've had for years, and like the intermittency of contractions, at times it was a painful process.

Your life can be compared to the construction site built around the womb to accommodate the dreams, but while you wait, your life is not on hold. However, just as with the natural birthing process, when the time comes to bring forth those dreams, plans, and visions, you need help to give birth—the right type of help.

I remember the words of a motivational speaker who said, "You may be busy pushing the dream, but don't forget the journey along the way." This is true because our lives are part of that journey, and, like money, we don't get the time back once it's spent. You will "give birth" at the right time and not before.

The Continuum

It took years of moving along the circular continuum of my life, a concept I described in chapter 4, to change a way of thinking I held so tightly. I'll briefly explain again what I define as "the continuum concept."

The Hebraic understanding of life is that it follows a circular, not linear, direction, meaning events come around, presenting "another" round of new opportunities. However, this time the experience—although different—presents another opportunity to approach the situation a different way for a better outcome. The question then becomes, how are you going to deal with the problem this time?

For years I grew comfortable with the problems I faced and enjoyed complaining, yet the predictability of my reaction consistently produced the same expected outcome. My husband is a badminton player, and after years of rejecting the sport, I decided to embrace it and learn to play. From the beginning, the game taught me that as long as you hit the shuttlecock with the same body positioning, it would fall in the same spot.

My thoughts felt like a badminton racket in my hand, poised to hit the shuttlecock (the problem) into the same area on the court with the same outcome. But it was time to break the cycle if I was ever going to realise the plans He had for me. Through life's everyday events, I allowed God to challenge me to acknowledge my strengths and difficulties, and soon I began to realise my strengths and areas of interest. I had no doubt my desires were synchronised with His.

Sometimes we try too hard to understand our purpose, but it's as simple as identifying areas of interest, setting related goals, and running with them. As you do that, your purpose becomes clearer as you work towards your goals. Eventually, we all have to stop talking and start doing—in the dark, silent place of the womb.

~

The Meaning of Mem

The ancient Hebrew representation for the letter *Mem* resembles waves of water, and its meaning relates to water, people, and nationalities. Its symbolic representation and meaning can also be seen as an "open" or "dilated" womb about to give birth. The letter Mem has the numerical value of forty and is linked to the twenty-second verse of Proverbs 31. It can be associated with hard testing. One biblical example is linked to the forty wilderness years the Hebrews were stuck in the same position due to an inability to trust God. Amongst other comparisons, it is also linked to the description of the great flood that lasted forty days when God protected a family but sent judgement to the rest of the world. During forty days of fasting, Jesus was tempted by Satan to move away from His Father's plan, but he did not give in.

Linked to many scriptures, the number forty has extremes: on one end, it signifies a time of suffering; on the other, giving birth, since the gestation period is forty weeks. Forty can also signify a time of accomplishment after days, months, or years of planning and working towards a goal. God accomplishes His plans in our lives. He makes visions a reality.

Clothes of Linen and Purple

Apart from silk, purple cloth was one of the most expensive materials. Linen was worn by the priests as a symbol of righteousness, representing right standing with God. During that time, linen was also worn by wealthy women as scarves. During a dark time in Jewish ancient history, the children of Israel worked as slaves in Egypt. It was there they—in particular the women—learned to make linen, as the Egyptians excelled in this area.[1] Much like the time it would have taken to source and weave the thread into linen, the Woman's wealth would have been "woven" over a period of time.

---

1. Elizabeth Fletcher, "Clothes in the Ancient Land of the Bible," Women in the Bible, October 25, 2022, http://www.womenintheBible.net/Bible-archaeology/clothes_ancient_Bible/.

God gives the dreams and passions we hold for our lives and works alongside us to realise our plans. When we finally see our hopes and dreams come alive after years of personal investment of time, prayer, emotions, and finance, the realisation eventually becomes a tangible achievement, and we can live it. God, through life experiences has been testing, shaping, building, and refining our characters so that when our lives align with God's set time to give birth to our plans, we effortlessly move to the next place in our lives. Circumstances may not always respect us as women, but they see our "clothes" —the linen, the silk and the wealth of God's presence on us— which is a powerful first impression.

Character Qualities

Father used many people to support and develop my character, and I firmly believe personalities are traits which separate one woman from another. For example, it may be our sense of humour, interests, the way we dress, or the scene we like to be part of that signals our individuality. I define "character qualities" as the strengths God wants to develop in us, such as showing kindness despite our feelings or not believing it's deserved, or exercising self-control when we want to explode. These responses reflect God's character qualities at work in us. As His Word says, "I can do all things through Christ who gives me strength." With only our own effort, this is hard, but it is God, through His Spirit, who strengthens us during these moments. The character strengths of silk and linen, woven over time, became the woman's strength. This is wealth because it produces and can't be taken away.

God in Us

Linen and purple clothing represent God's presence in everyday events. His presence is His life, weaving through ours with the support we need on a daily basis. The description of the Woman's clothes symbolises Father's presence in her life, and we use the Word to call on God's strength every day, starting like this:

> **"O Lord, hear me as I pray; pay attention to my groaning. Listen to my cry for help, my King and my God, for I pray to no one but you. Listen to my voice in the morning, Lord. Each morning I bring my requests to you and wait expectantly."**
>
> **—Psalms 5:1–3**

This verse directs our call to God, the Head and Strong Leader of our lives, long before the day begins. We shape the day with the words we use, and when we speak God's Words, we are speaking life into the twenty-four hours. Whichever way I look at these words, they speak of the need to push deeper into God, particularly when life is tough, because we need His protection and ability.

Like the woman's linen scarf, we need God's covering of Shalom and His righteousness on our heads—the place where we house all our thoughts, the ones that come to us last thing at night and stand at the door of our mind first thing in the morning. Our heads are the place of our creativity, our future, plans, and dreams. It is the place that builds our character and drives our actions. In hindsight, I now know it was Father's covering that healed my mental health on that grey day as I pushed my son in his buggy, counting doors while an internal discussion burned in my head.

The Silence of the Womb

There is a place in our lives where God has chosen to work, and it's the place where He works best. However, it's a place we see as dark and hidden. It's like a void, deeply embedded, without shape or movement—like a building site without materials. When we can't see the direction of where we are going or the turns life is about to take, we may feel as though nothing is happening or, better still, nothing wants to happen. Then there's a sense that all creative ability has drained away with plans and ideas scattered. Encouraging words spoken into our lives vaporise, and the people we look to for encouragement are gone. It appears life has watched us a thousand times over as we agonise and watch the scene replay often and perfectly. We plan for things to happen; we expect progress. Yet the dream seems distant, and everything moves slowly. Then, on some days, time appears to stop, and we scroll through the lives of others. This is a time in an environment I like to describe as "the silence of the womb."

The writings in Psalms 139 (CJB) paint a vivid picture of God at work in the womb as we watch the seemingly endless cycle of "no progress" replay. However, just like the developing child in the womb, our plans are being formed perfectly in the quiet of the womb. Be patient because as you wait, you will see and feel the baby kick; the plan is in progress!

"For you fashioned my inmost being, you knit me together in my mother's womb. I thank you because I am awesomely made, wonderfully;

your works are wonders —I know this very well. My bones were not hidden from you when I was being made in secret, intricately woven in the depths of the earth. Your eyes could see me as an embryo, but in your book all my days were, already written; my days had been shaped before any of them existed. God, how I prize your thoughts! How many of them there are! If I count them, there are more than grains of sand; if I finish the count, I am still with you."

—Psalm 139:13–18 CJB

Womb Women

Father is developing His character qualities in us so that we can handle our dreams when they come. When that time arrives, I don't believe we'll be perfect, but we will have enough of what we need to manage the magnitude of the dreams we nurtured for years. Father sent many women into my life to help develop the dreams I carried. They were dissimilar in personality and sometimes the very opposite of the women I would choose to be around. But likeable or not, I realised God had sent them to sharpen me. When I realised the work Father was doing, I saw it as an opportunity to observe, listen, and develop in order to change. Often, the encounters were brief—a few months, a year or two—yet on time for that phase of my life, and I hope I had something to give to them. Sometimes I wanted the friendships to continue, but they slowly fizzled out, and Father would remind me He had placed those women in my life for a season.

I recall the encouraging words from one of my "womb women" during a fleeting moment of self-doubt. Those words came to me, as the scriptures describe it, "like a custom-made piece of jewellery," perfectly suited for the occasion.

As a speech and language therapist, I regularly train senior management, school staff, and parents. This occasion, however, was different; I was about to give a presentation to parents and staff that, based on new research, I hoped would shift existing concepts of language development.

Before leaving my office, I prayed, as I always do, that Father would help me to present with clarity whilst being aware of the many concerns and anxieties parents hold when children are born with significant communication needs. Father swiftly reminded me of a message a friend had sent a few weeks earlier: "He (Father) always comes through. All will be well because you are gifted to do what you do." Gathering my notes, I walked toward the packed room, feeling strengthened by the encouraging words from this womb woman. The presentation was successful; unusually, many parents cried with relief and asked questions. This outcome had been spurred along by my womb woman.

I have many stories of beautiful women who have supported me over the years with prayer, giving time to listen, meals, and financial and professional advice. They have counselled, encouraged, cried, and laughed with me. It is experiences like these that carve character and shape every area of our lives. On the difficult days, we emerge stronger and wealthier in experience, mind, and spirit from the support of women God sends into our lives!

Not surprisingly, in agreement with the Proverb that states, "As a man (woman) thinks in his (her) heart so is he (she)," a healthy mind, spirit, and emotions are the basis for what we produce every day. Now wealthier in experience, mind, and spirit, the

Woman in 31 is experiencing the vision she has been working towards during the long days and nights she spent weaving the quilt of her plans with Father present in her life at each step.

In the first chapter, I spoke about God as the Aleph, the Strong Leader of our lives who gives identity. During tough times or dark days when we most want to be held, covered and sheltered like a baby in the womb, God gives us the strength of His character to be able to handle those times and manage them well.

"For I can do everything through Christ who gives me strength."

—Philippians 4:13

We Will Give Birth to Our Dreams

As I explained earlier, the number for Mem is forty and, amongst other biblical references, is the number of the gestational period for giving birth. The letter also symbolises water and a womb about to give birth. God has promised we will give birth to our dreams; it's just a matter of timing, patience, and persistence. It's during the season of waiting that God develops character that cannot be broken, only built. Like the womb, the dream or plans—whatever you choose to call them—seem to be in a dark place; then there are days, even months and years when you wonder whether they will ever happen. As you battle with the "Will it ever happen?" thoughts, I encourage you to trust God and learn to trust Him daily.

Don't Worry

Developing a consistent attitude of trust is a process that doesn't happen overnight. However, being prepared to trust is all Father—the Strong Leader of our lives—wants in order to move us through difficult times. In Genesis chapter 1, the Bible talks about the "evening" and the "morning" being the first day. If we think about and understand that statement, we realise it explains that night comes before day. In Jewish understanding, a new day begins at sundown. So, for example, the 5th of November would start on the evening of the 4th. The day always begins with night. This is consistent with Genesis 1, verse 5, which says:

"...The evening and the morning were the first day."

The latter part of Psalm 30, verse 5 encourages:

"Weeping may last through the night, but joy comes with the morning."

The womb is a dark place, but everything is set up for the developing baby. The pain comes first, then joy, and we forget the pain. Using the womb as an analogy, dreams and plans sometimes seem in a dark place, but Father can be trusted to deliver on His promises and will lead through those dark days. The psalmist in chapter 139 says, "Even darkness is light to Him." I can honestly say that I lived through what seemed like long years of darkness, and it was during those years I chose to turn to God and trust that He would clothe me in linen and purple like the Woman in 31.

Two Wombs, Two Women

The Bible describes two women on a journey, separated by age and experience. The first is a woman called Sarah. She's a mature woman, well into her seventies, with many stories to tell from her life journeys. We learn Sarah was confident, intelligent, and a devoted wife who was also described as visually beautiful. As a young woman, her expectation was to marry and have a family, meeting the cultural normalities of her time. However, years later, her outward body and visual image changed; more crucially, her reproductive cycle was ending as the new Woman emerged. The changes her body made were not late, but for Sarah, they challenged her hope of ever having a child.

However, time has moved on and now Sarah has matured beyond her reproductive years. Her body has bowed to the laws of time and age, and now her outward body and visual image has changed. Perhaps, like many women in a difficult phase of life she has asked the question: *Is there still hope for me?*

Life was not going as planned, and eventually, she gave up on her dreams. Then at the well-seasoned age of eighty-nine, God answered her prayers and promised she would have a child. Years continued to pass. Her menstrual cycles stopped as her body entered its transition for the next phase of her journey. The hope buried deep in Sarah's "womb" seemed to die. Desperate to have a child, desperate to not see her desire to become a mother to her own children die, and desperate to have her husband's name continue, Sarah took drastic action, but not without lifelong consequences.

Centuries later, a woman called Mary was born into the same culture. She was young—scholars cite her age as maybe fifteen

—and engaged to a man named Joseph. As with Sarah, Mary's expectation was to get married and have children; she was able to have a family with no worries about age stopping the process. Then, according to God's plan, He spoke to Mary through the angel Gabriel, and she became pregnant supernaturally without sleeping with Joseph.

Comparing Sarah and Mary's experiences, both women would have been the subject of gossip: Mary's pregnancy outside of marriage and Sarah's inability to have children. Although Sarah was a beautiful woman and loved by her husband, her inevitable future was no child and no legacy. However, both women held onto the vision in their wombs that God had given them, determined to produce their dreams and see the reality of the promises. Despite the shame and embarrassment and, in Mary's case, the near break-up of her engagement (even though no physical relationship had taken place), they continued to move forward.

Dealing with the Emotion of Shame

At this stage of writing, it's difficult to move forward without returning to the toxic emotion called shame. The ability to open up and talk about shame is important because it holds so many women captive and seeks to destroy their wombs and dreams—the very essence of who they are. Every time you move forward, shame wants to pierce your mind and hold you trapped in its darkness. Shame is a hidden feeling, eating away on the inside, invisible to others. It is a painful and grievous trial, digging deep, dark, cavernous pits into the lives it grasps. Skilfully masked, we learn to live with it until we allow Father to expose the feeling for what it is by identifying its roots and allowing Him to heal us.

However, God asks:

> **"'Shall I bring to the time of birth, and not cause delivery?' says the Lord. 'Shall I who cause delivery shut up *the womb?*' says your God."**
>
> **—Isaiah 66:9–10 NKJV**

God is making it clear that He sees the end from the beginning and will deliver on His promises. His work (our plans) stays hidden inside our "wombs," away from all to see—even ourselves—until the right time arrives.

The womb vision carries much responsibility and waiting time, but the outcome will impact lives on a scale not accomplished by others because every child from the womb is different in personality, character, and appearance. It may be true that "Everyone has a story to tell," but your story will not have the same details and information as another woman. It's impossible. Ideas are being realised, and innovation is happening right there in the womb where no one can see. You're the woman, the innovator, carrying the responsibility for nurturing the creation, desire, dream, plans, and the increasing responsibility of the project as it matures. So, enjoy the journey to the realisation of the vision; it's part of the process of development.

Chapter 14

The Process of Healing

NUN
Her husband is known at the city gates
when he sits with the leaders of the land.

After years of Father building my life, He allowed me to experience a second chance. His grace is sufficient for everything, but the building and shaping continued in my marriage with Andrew. The premise of our marriage is friendship and a covenant we made before God. I had often heard people describe the "friendship" part; however, I often believed it was simply a well-used term couples applied to define their relationship. Andrew and I were friends long before we married. We could laugh and talk for hours and just enjoyed each other's company. Our relationship was formed from how we enjoyed going for drives, listening to music, and finding quiet places to park, eat, and talk (or say nothing). Then there were many times when the car became a quiet space to work through our problems. Partnerships, formed friendships leading to marriage covenants, are built on the ability to listen, apologise, and laugh. The third dimension, as I describe it, is the core of our marriage covenant: faith and prayer. These are the disciplines that continue to build our marriage.

Although heard often, I really don't like the word "institution," meaning a societal "tradition" or "custom" used as a description for marriage. Traditions and outlooks change with time; consequently, the definition shifts and is redefined away from its original design. Marriage is based on a covenant between God and His people. God's marriage covenant is founded on His instructions and promises, which don't change as society's values shift. When making promises, we exchange words that set mutual expectations based on God's instructions for marriage, which become the foundation.

People are free to define and shape their expectations of marriage in any area of belief they choose, but God's marriage covenant and the scriptures, which guide our lives, are written in His Words for life. He says, "I am the Lord, and I don't change." (Malachi 3:6) People break covenants, not God, although He extends His hands to us, again and again, to help us keep our side of the promise. My Dad often explained, "Marriages break down when one or both parties choose to reject God's instructions for the individual to keep the covenant." Although I experienced this during my first marriage, I learned God is forgiving and faithful, and His Words energise when we read and apply them to life.

Andrew and I married in 2006 after years of allowing God to help make our lives a whole picture from what looked like fragments. The engagement journey up until that point had been amazing despite the many times I thought we would never make it. He was dealing with his own issues, and I mine.

But when we got together, the developing strong bonds of friendship and honesty about what we wanted in life was enough to commit to the next stage. Andrew kept his promise to Sam and me, and I to him. Then, on the 9th of September, we were married in the small church in East London where I had watched Samuel grow up and where we met to support our spiritual growth.

September

The sunny September autumn morning of this wedding was different than the first wedding, and I was different. God, over time, had healed painful memories. This time, I had complete confidence in the commitment I was about to make.

I chose to wear a fifties-style wedding dress with a beaded bodice and multi-layered tulle designed to bounce and float off the mid-length raw silk ivory skirt. My aunt and I bought the fabric in a shop at the end of London's Berwick Street Market, which was popular with fashion and theatre designers. It was exciting seeing rolls of fabric in an array of colours waiting to be shaped and cut. Growing up, my aunt made many of my clothes, and I always loved the idea of transforming fabric into the many designs I drew on paper. She was a master with the scissors, and to this day, she continues to sew for her many clients. My aunt's second and final contribution to my married life was about to take place, and—after years of shaping—like the woman in 31, I was about to be dressed in my own "linen and purple."

This time it was my sisters, Leah and Georgia, who helped me slip into my beautiful handmade wedding dress. I remember my feet sinking into the deep, piled, soft green bedroom carpet as I moved around the room in excitement, trying to be as calm as possible. This time it was different. This time the future was based on the foundation of the experiences life had created, and Andrew was a man I had watched God craft over the years. This was the realisation of the "foundation of sapphires" that Father had first mentioned years ago. This time, I was a mature woman with a son, who was becoming a young man. That required a different parenting style, and Andrew was about to learn how to work alongside Sam as we became a blended family.

The First Five Years

Unsurprisingly, the first five years of our marriage were about learning to live together and further exploring through thought processes, attitudes, strengths, and needs and learning about the spiritual aspects of each other's lives. Those years taught us how to manage time, relationships, prayer, money, home, health, and our ongoing personal development. There were rocky moments, but never for long because we had invested the early years of our friendship in developing a mutual understanding. We were also tracing the shapes God was drawing into our new family, with Andrew having to learn how to parent a teenage boy. Although Andrew had watched Sam grow, now living in the home, my husband brought a new dynamic to the relationship while Sam was discovering his identity as a young man. We didn't have the experience of knowing what to do or how to develop the new family that was forming. But despite the challenges, the family relationship strengthened and grew organically on God's Words.

∼

The Meaning of Nun

Linked to the twenty-third verse, the number for the Hebrew letter *Nun* (pronounced "noon") is fifty and means "life" and "restoration." The source of both is God's Holy Spirit, restoring and giving life to everything He touches in us. Historical representations of the letter Nun looked like a sperm, which symbolises the life carried by men. Nun also means an anointing (God's presence with us), as we read when Mary, Yeshua's (Jesus') mother, was anointed by God's Spirit to give birth to His Son.

As we read in the Gospels, Christ was anointed to carry out His work for the planned short time He was here. The reference to the Woman's husband then reminds us that her life comes from God. I am talking now about God's life to us as Women, married and single, and the head of the Woman is Christ. His life moves through us to give life to our own through His continual presence with us—who we know is His Holy Spirit—energising and giving us direction. Irrespective of the work husbands do or the positions they hold, God sustains the couple because He is the Head of our lives. The man and woman work together, following God's original design and description in Genesis, while humbling themselves to one another as Paul advised. Every couple will pattern their marriages according to what they understand from the scriptures. As you can deduce from what I'm writing, there is a lot to say here, which is not the subject of this book.

Nun is the fourteenth number position in the Hebrew alphabet and means to rescue from harm, ruin, or loss. Matthew chapter 1, verse 17, counts fourteen generations from Abraham to David, fourteen from David to the exile in Babylon, and fourteen from the exile to Christ's time. Relating that number to my life, I was surprised to discover that, since leaving home to get married in 1988, I had moved fourteen times, renting and experiencing home ownership. During those fourteen years since leaving home to get married in 1988 to now, Father has been there, constantly *rescuing* me in different ways.

At this point in our journey, the Woman in 31 is now experiencing the many years and months spent planning, designing, and discussing. She is watching the plans she made come alive. The fact that she is running her own business suggests that her plans are succeeding; she is increasing on all levels and is able to meet her needs and those of her family. You could look at this description from many angles, but whatever your perspective or interpretation, it points to the same conclusion: her vision, no matter how long it took, has become a reality.

There is a cycle in our lives where we become productive as the ideas, dreams, plans, and visions become real. It's about production. Trust, or placing our faith in God, allows our lives to move forward; whatever the pace, we make progress. The Hebrew word for trust is *emunah*. Broken down into its Hebrew letters, it means the ability to trust in the character of God, the One who made the promise. This is not trusting in the promise on its own but placing trust in God, who is able to make good on His Words.

Emunah comes from the word *aman* (from which we get the word "amen"), an affirmative which means to securely trust or rely. We never take what is sometimes described as "a leap of faith" without a basis for the decision. We make plans. God gives us those desires, and we pray, take advice from others, research, and move ahead. God promises He will make plans successful, and based on his faithful and trustworthy character, we push forward with both hands. We trust the One who is able to deliver. We trust in God to *do* what he says.

Number 93

A year before we moved into 93, a day before my birthday, Father showed me another dream where I saw that we were about to experience a very difficult time. However, He gave His word that He would not only lead us through but also help us understand the way He works in our lives. In the summer of that year, Andrew was made redundant from his job, and we spent a few edgy months waiting to hear details of his redundancy package. It was soon evident that he would be out of work by the end of August that year with a small package compared to how long he had spent at the organisation. Without obvious worry, Andrew felt confident he would soon get work as an IT contractor due to his level of experience, so we took a short break abroad.

Three months later, in November, Andrew was still out of work. Financial commitments had started to mount, and we were beginning to experience tough times. To remind myself of what God had promised, I searched for the dream I had written in my diary and read it again. It was now clear we had entered that phase. We had anticipated staying only a short while at 93 to build finances and buy a home within twenty-four months. We spoke to Father about our plans and knew He had heard. As our situation deepened, we began to realise that one of His purposes was to help us gain a concrete understanding of our faith by reviewing the "what" and the "why." In other words, what we do and why we do it. We started to understand the

Bible in what I describe as 3-dimensional. Above all, God was teaching us to trust Him.

For me, this process began a long time before my dad had passed, as I was trying to reconcile what I had been taught. It was, if you like, an "audit," and I wasn't afraid to look at the results, as I wanted answers. Before Dad passed, I spent time with him discussing, questioning, and reasoning as I struggled to find answers for the difficult processes. But I knew God was always listening, and He would answer.

On a dark winter's morning in November, I leaned against the worktop, crying in the kitchen of the new apartment. I sensed we were about to experience our first very tough challenge. I felt angry and at a loss concerning what the months would bring. I didn't want any more struggle.

My Dad transitioned in circumstances I would not have imagined, and I hadn't yet addressed the emotional strain it had taken on my life. I hadn't considered the surreal events of having to drive with my brother John to the local shops holding the regular, necessary prescription for morphine. The bright November day captured the conversation of shoppers and people enjoying the last rays of the sun. The sounds and sights remained suspended in the atmosphere long enough for John and me to listen to normality against the backdrop of the situation facing Dad and the family. The Saturday market stalls, selling a rich variety of homemade foods, lined the side of the road, hiding the local shops, and the relaxed scene struck a sharp contrast to how we felt as we walked to the counter to hand over the prescription, like money, in exchange for a powerful drug to dull the physical pain. Deep down, though, in the sadness of my soul, there was still hope that although Dad was going, it wouldn't be the end. That's the difference: we have hope in Christ Jesus.

Years later, on the anniversary of his passing, I watched a clean white transit van drive past my parent's home as I sat waiting in the car for my mother. I was surprised to notice the private number plate, unusual for a white van, which read "George d." My father's name was George, and I took the "d" for "dad." As on many previous occasions, I believe this was a smile from God and an affirmation that all was well and we would see him again.

We moved into number 93 the day before my birthday, and the next morning, with the cautionary dream fresh in my mind, there I stood, crying in the kitchen. It may have been a combination of thoughts. Andrew was still out of work, and we were managing on one income, and there I was, experiencing yet another move in my life. I was tired and angry with God; my emotions were in conflict with what we believed God had shown about our future. He had shown us on many occasions and in so many ways that He would prosper us in every way. But on that cold, dark 17th day in November, the morning of my birthday, it was hard to trust; it was hard to believe, and I felt numb. Where was God in all of this? Where was my life going? It was all a mess.

Before Christmas 2011, with savings now dangerously low, Andrew was offered a short contract. It was just enough to meet our bills and household expenses until January of the following year when I would get funds into my business. And as in the small things, we learned God was able to meet our needs. The contract came at the right time, as Andrew was beginning to get discouraged by sitting at home all day waiting for agencies to call with contracts that never materialised. Recalling the many interviews Andrew had with no success, we recognised God was with us throughout. While we were in this tough "desert" place, He used the time to build our character and trust and to meet our daily needs, just as Apostle Paul stated: "But my God shall supply all your need according to His riches in glory by Christ Jesus" (Philippians 4:19 KJV). And then further along, in James 1:2–4, it says:

> **"Dear brothers and sisters, when troubles of any kind come your way, consider it an opportunity for great joy. For you know that when your faith is tested, your endurance has a chance to grow. So let it grow, for when your endurance is fully developed, you will be perfect and complete, needing nothing."**

After this short four-week contract, we were hopeful another would immediately follow. While we waited, we kept our minds and spirits up by reading scriptures, praying, and discussing at length the importance of strong relationships between family and friends during difficult times.

By the next year, finances severely depleted and emotionally drained, we were at a very low point. We felt alone and isolated. Saturday morning, I woke up with a sinking feeling about the dark turn of events and decided to escape to the shopping centre for a coffee. Just as I left the tunnel leading to the motorway I started crying as I began to question God about our dire situation. *Where were His blessings? What had I done wrong? What about all the time and effort I had made for others, and now, when I needed help, there was no one?* As I drove along the motorway crying, I heard God's gentle voice giving practical advice.

"You can do one of two things: either drive crying, which is not safe, or pull over and then cry."

What a shock! I chose to stop crying and immediately heard the calming words float quietly into my mind: "The Lord is my Shepherd; I have all that I need." The words grasped my emotions and were comforting, and as soon as I reached the next available junction, I turned the car around and drove in the direction of where I needed to be.

Later that day, I found a document online about the 23rd Psalm, and, for the first time, it presented the Psalm in a way I hadn't understood, which was amazing! This was Father's first introduction to us discovering our faith in a tangible way. That day marked the beginning of a deepening understanding of the Bible in a practical, life-application way. Studying the document, we began to understand more of what it meant to allow God to be "the Shepherd of our lives," that He was the one leading us, and if we were to experience life, as in Nun, we were to follow and *trust* His leadership. Later that month we found another document describing the covenants upon which all of God's promises are based.

In the months that followed, we remained hopeful despite no work. Interviews with promises of contracts came and went, leaving us with nothing but empty discussions. Still, we continued to trust. What we didn't realise, however, was that God was showing us how to experience the reality of *emunah* (trust) by experiencing His Words through everyday life. Andrew's lack of work challenged us to the core of our belief. It forced us to address the question, *Will God answer?* Did we pray to a God who didn't hear or wasn't able to listen? His words through the prophet Isaiah challenge this line of thinking: "Listen! The Lord's arm is not too weak to save you, nor is his ear too deaf to hear you call." (Isaiah 59:1) Then in the New Testament, Philippians chapter 4, verses 6 and 7, instruct us not to worry but to pray about everything, and God will give us peace.

We were learning the basics and foundation of God's instructions to put our trust in the strength of His character while doing what we needed to get back into employment and rebuild our finances. Finally, after a fairly long telephone interview, Andrew was offered a short contract in Jersey, an Island off the UK. He was given an immediate start date on the Monday following the weekend. All the documents were sent over as requested, and Andrew was packed and ready. Then on the Friday morning before the Monday he was due to travel, the call came to say the client had cancelled the contract. That afternoon, Andrew drove to pick me up from work. The drive refocused him and provided a mental break from the demanding job search.

It was the end of a long working week, and I had left for work that morning, relieved at the news that Andrew was back in employment and we would soon have money to pay the bills and get on with life. After throwing the heavy work bags into the car boot, I opened the door, sat, and turned to him. His expression told me what I didn't want to hear. We were devastated, as funds were critically low.

The usual drive over London's famous Tower Bridge, always vibrant with tourists, lights, and the sound of the river boats, seemed dull and slow this time. It seemed to match a rainy Monday afternoon. As I watched the many people stopping to frame their lives in pictures and walk and view the London sights along the river, I couldn't help but wonder what *their* lives were like. I took a snapshot with my own mental camera to see whether anyone behind the smiles had experienced the same as us. And if not, I imagined myself asking, *Can I share my story?* By the time we drove through a tunnel leading to the short drive home, I was so broken that I put my face in my hands and cried out of frustration and disappointment. I later realised that God sometimes uses the circumstances of life to push us to the edge of reason, then to the bleeding edge, until there's nowhere left to stand! And just as it seems we would plunge into the precipice, the edge disappears, and we fly! But the edge disappears, and then we fly.

Sometime later, in the spring and summer of 2012, God began to give us the understanding of the Judeo-Christian roots of our faith, which made us review what we believed and why we believed it. It was like having continuing professional development for our faith. What we discovered was astounding, and we wished we had understood it years before. We read the Bible and searched for the Hebraic environmental context of its description. We explored the understanding of the Hebrew idioms, customs, and the linguistic structure of words to enrich the meaning of the text, which gave a clearer picture of how this applied to our lives. There isn't the capacity in this book to talk about that journey, but suffice it to say, equipped with the tools to apply the understanding to our everyday lives, we began to see results. Over time, we were able to cross off prayer requests as God began to answer them one by one.

The sweltering summer continued with emotional and money challenges. Still, despite the desperate situation, we were happy and hungry for more understanding of our faith, and this desire was deepening the relationship we knew with God. Knowledge is great, but the question we need to ask is, *What's the outcome?* Is the knowledge helping us to understand God's ways more, or is it just knowledge for knowledge's sake?

The summer heat intensified, and the apartment became a furnace, as the building had been designed to store heat—preferably in the winter. We would sit fanning late into the night on deckchairs we had borrowed from family, which we used in the absence of furniture. For relief we spent most evenings walking to the river near where we lived and up onto the bridge. After climbing the fifty or so metal steps leading to the top, the view was stunning! The brightly coloured mix of lights from the boats on the marina, the hotels, restaurants, and houses lining the river's edge all shimmered and floated over the river. And as we sat at the top gazing at the scene, time kindly stopped to give us time to think.

Summer turned to autumn and then winter. No work. The new year, 2013, came and with it—just after celebrating Passover—God's Words to us from the book of Hosea. We sensed God was confirming that it was time to "get to work because He was with us." I prayed while Andrew was in a telephone interview with a company based overseas and then read from the scriptures—where God gave me the words that Andrew would "succeed." I was confident then that he was going to get this contract. When the interview ended, Andrew felt he did well, but after so many experiences, we didn't get excited; we simply trusted God. The call came later that afternoon: the company wanted to interview him a second time. *Could this be the one?* But we were so focused and trusting in the words God had said since, over the last eighteen months, we had learned much about aspects of God's character moving us to trust.

On the morning of the second interview, Andrew wore one of his best suits. We specifically asked Father the colour of the shirt and tie. Of course, that's not the way we usually decide on clothes and God doesn't expect us to! But, for that moment, we wanted to involve Him in the smallest details of our lives because that's how we were able to stay focused during those eighteen months. Otherwise, we would have been crushed mentally and emotionally.

We drove to the location and found a parking space a few minutes walk from the building where he was going for his interview. I waited in the car, listening to one of my Dad's last messages he spoke to the church called "Get out of the Box!" It was so relevant for the time we were in because he taught about trust and changing the way we think. After listening to the message, I put some music on and waited.

On that bright, spring day, around 3:30 in the afternoon, I clearly heard God's voice instructing me to stop listening and pray because Andrew was being asked some very difficult questions. Twenty minutes later he returned, opened the car door, took off his jacket, sat down and put his face in his hands, and I just knew, even though he hadn't said a word.

"Well, how did you get on?"

I heard his words before he moved his mouth, "I got it!"

The interview *was* tough, but he felt confident in his responses. Then, just as he was about to drive away from the office, the interviewer called him back inside and asked him to take a seat and wait for a few moments while he left the room. Those "few moments" seemed like forever, as Andrew would later explain. The interviewer re-entered the room, sat down behind the desk, and asked Andrew to "name his salary!" Father had taught us to trust Him, and He did not disappoint.

God took us through many dark, potentially depressing, and worrying days which could have crushed our faith, but He had taught us how to trust Him. Then like the letter Nun, His life enabled ours. The experience was extremely dark at times, like the moment in the kitchen where we stood facing each other, and Andrew spoke honestly about his fear of never re-entering his profession as he had been out for a long while. The IT industry is constantly changing, at least every eighteen months, which was equal to the time Andrew had been out of contract. But God heard and was present to teach and meet our needs. He taught us that He is the Aleph, the Strong Leader and Head of our Home.

Jesus Christ revealed Himself to us in a deeper way. We stopped going through the religious motions where you risk repeating the same routines and behaviours without engaging in the real questions. Our faith became deeper and more meaningful, and just as the way a husband and wife get to know each other over the years, we got to know God more.

Later that year, Andrew was assigned to a project based in Johannesburg, South Africa, and we continued to move in the direction God wanted for our lives. I moved from a place of fighting with doubt and levels of insecurities to increased stability and confidence. In the same year, we bought furniture for our home; small steps, but for us, this was a luxury. God proved we could trust Him throughout all the difficult circumstances we faced during those eighteen months, and He opened "gates," i.e., opportunities, that were closed to us. This is further supported in Isaiah 45, verse 2, where it says: "I will go before you...and will level the mountains; I will smash down gates of bronze and cut through bars of iron." (This, of course, is multi-layered in meaning.)

I have just described events marking a significant stage in my life. The events represent another level of growth in my character, and I began to make further progress. Now having a new understanding of God's ways and how He worked in my life, I was able to move beyond mere theology.

Difficult experiences carried an opportunity to build character and watch progress. Then, like the Woman in 31, my life slowly became a cycle of greater production, and I began to see the outcome of the plans I had made. It didn't happen all at once, although over time, some things became evident. I compare my life to a building under construction, and now I am learning to appreciate what God is doing even though I can't always understand the process.

Chapter 15

Inner Healing

SAMEKH and AYIN
She makes linen garments and sells them;
she supplies the merchants with sashes.
Clothed with strength and dignity
she can laugh at the days to come.

While working towards future goals, many of us spend much of our time dealing with simmering emotions. These emotions, when left unchecked, affect our everyday lives. They can skew our perspectives, hinder our progress, and even manifest as physical ailments. Therefore, inner healing becomes not just a necessity but a critical part of our journey towards personal growth and fulfilment.

Part of the ability of being able to laugh at the days to come stems from the process of inner healing. It is through this process of healing that we are able to reconcile with our past, manage our present, and build a healthier, more resilient future. Inner healing allows us to face our emotions head-on, understand their roots, and eventually move beyond them, enabling us to pursue our goals with greater clarity, determination, and peace of mind. But first, we must recognise the presence of these hindering emotions, uncovering the masks they so often cower behind.

Have you ever second-guessed your decisions and failed to grasp opportunities presented to help you move to your next stage? Are you hiding behind some of your best work due to an irrational fear that the activity or content is not good enough? Have you ever held back during a meeting, hesitant to speak up for fear your ideas may be dismissed? Do you constantly worry people are judging you and assume their thoughts about you are negative? Would you rather "fit in" with the crowd than stand out? Most of us would respond with a resounding "Yes!" to one, if not all, of the above. Each of these scenarios, as well as others, are subtle clues that inner healing is needed. Experiences of crushing rejection, episodes of low self-esteem, and lack of confidence plagued my early years. This was particularly true during the time I tried to revive my first marriage, but by then, it was too late. Journey with me to a time before I met Andrew as we revisit the point in time where I became aware of my own need for inner healing.

Artificial Light

My working day placed the baton firmly into the hands of the afternoon routine, and I followed its familiar steps to the nursery. Scooping up my son for the long-awaited, end-of-the-day hug, I then fitted him into his all-in-one thermal coat and covered his curly brown hair with his woolly hat. We were now ready to drive home, but not before a quick trip to the local supermarket. That particular area of East London always felt familiar as it triggered distant happy memories of joint shopping trips with my then-husband, his sister, and brother-in-law years earlier. We were a young couple whose conversations were always full of excitement and optimism when we talked about future plans. Years later my then sister-in-law and her family left East London to start a new chapter in a leafy-green affluent suburb.

The shopping mall was the first of its kind and one of many large, out-of-town supermarkets that quickly became part of the UK shopping experience. The chrome lining of the new food counters shone with the bright expectation of receiving a flood of shoppers with their supermarket trolleys stacked with food items. And the supermarket aisles that appeared to stretch for miles framed the lanes with neatly stacked tins and boxes.

Fast forward nine years, and I am now a young mum, shopping in the same supermarket, pushing the trolley down the same aisles. But, just like my life, the shine of the once vibrant new store had since dulled and become weighted with years of stories to tell.

There I was, back in East London, after starting a new life in a situation that wasn't anywhere in the plans we made back then. I was determined to make the best of my life as it was and push forward. And as I recounted earlier, somewhere buried in the back of my mind, I hoped my husband and I would be able to heal our marriage.

I watched my son's little feet toddling ahead of me in his all-in-one, red and blue toddler coat. The heavy padding had saved him on the few occasions when he had decided to throw himself backwards onto the supermarket floor in a temper tantrum at the store entrance. This was an amusing new phase in his development, and that day was no different. As he lay on the floor, I looked at him and smiled as he stared back at me. Game over, drama over, and the shopping now done, the supermarket trolley, Sam and I reached the tills.

It had been a long day, and I was tired and looking forward to packing the shopping into the boot of the car for the short drive home. I pushed the trolley to the counter and started to stack the groceries on the conveyor belt, poised to make the quick move to the other end to pack. Then I had a surreal moment. For some reason I glanced down at my wedding band with its slight indent to fit the engagement ring. The diamonds had caught the artificial supermarket light and were reflecting in all directions. It was then I realised it was hopeless; the marriage was over, and I would be bringing up my son alone.

In that moment it was as though the store had shortened its aisles and lowered the ceiling, all the shoppers had turned to face me, and everyone knew what I was desperately trying to ignore. That poignant moment was a clear indication of permanent change. I discreetly slid the rings from my finger and placed them carefully in my inside jacket pocket then continued packing as I fought to hold back the tears. Unbeknownst to me, the long process of healing had begun.

The Meaning of Samekh

Samekh, the fifteenth letter of the Hebrew alphabet with a number value of sixty, is paired with the twenty-fourth verse of Proverbs. The meaning of Samekh is understood as "to lean upon," "to twist or turn slowly" or "to support." It also is linked to the concept of transferring something through touch. The letter meaning "support" is saying God's presence is the shelter in our lives.

Clothes

How many times have we stressed about an event, interview, or business meeting we needed to attend, with all-consuming thoughts about what to wear? Besides the primary purpose of covering our bodies, clothes can be used as a strong signal to present aspects of our identity wrapped in personality and emotions. They are often the first impression given at first glance, and ideas are formed from how we present.

The Woman's clothes, in this verse, could represent the inner covering of God's strength of character and dignity. It would have taken time to "dress" the Woman, many years of building her "strength," restoring "dignity," and healing her emotions to reach a level of confidence where she was relaxed, productive, and able to "laugh at the days to come."

Part of being able to "laugh at the days to come" stems from the *process* of inner healing. Building up a wardrobe of clothes takes money, investment, time, trial and error, organising, and clearing out the old to bring in the new, comparable to building character. There is a cost to the process. In reality, we're not often laughing at the days to come. Instead, those days find us off track, worrying, watching other people's lives, feeling inadequate, and wondering if our situation is ever going to change. Through our daily life experiences, we must allow God to take his time to dress us with His clothes as we lean on or trust Him. As a guideline for prayer, in Matthew 6, verse 11 (NIV), Jesus taught, "Give us today our daily bread." In this instance we can take that to mean "Give me the strength and dignity I need today." In other words, Father, clothe me.

Dignity

The concept of "dignity" comes from a word with multi-layered applications. The word dignity is defined as the "state" or "quality" of being worthy of honour and respect. It could be described as a core value in how we see ourselves. In some cases, we will fight to protect our dignity through actions to gain recognition and respect. Without a sense of dignity, a woman is vulnerable and unable to merit her rights. We see then, like the description of the Woman in 31, that being covered in dignity can be compared to wearing clothes to protect our vulnerability and sense of self.

"Dignity" has the connotation of maturity, gentleness, wisdom, and integrity. The ability to wear this type of clothing comes from experience and is worn with God's grace. I define wisdom as "applying what has been learned to every new situation." Having said that, most would agree that maturity and wisdom are not default buttons that come with age but the ability to allow God to work through the challenges we face in our lives and learn from them in some way.

I have met women in their early twenties and thirties who have shown maturity far greater than their age, probably because they've learned from mistakes, applied what they learned to new situations, and moved forward. The clothes of "strength" and "dignity" are then qualities which can only be carved from experience and application, allowing women to face the future with confidence despite how they feel. Thankfully, God's clothes always fit.

The Meaning of Ayin

Seventy is the value of the next Hebrew letter, *Ayin*, the sixteenth letter along the alphabet. Its number is linked to "order," "restoration in its fullness," and "perfection." Ayin is linked to the twenty-fifth verse. Early drawings of the letter resembled an "eye," and the letter represents "eye" or "to see," "understand," or "grasp."

In the book of Matthew, Yeshua talks about having the ability to "see" and "hear" on a spiritual level in order to make practical life changes. Here is an excerpt of what Jesus was explaining:

> **"When you hear what I say, you will not understand. When you see what I do, you will not comprehend. For the hearts of these people are hardened, and their ears cannot hear, and they have closed their eyes—so their eyes cannot see, and their ears cannot hear, and their hearts cannot understand, and they cannot turn to me and let me heal them."**
>
> **—Matthew 13:14–15**

Here, Jesus was quoting from the Prophet Isaiah. Father wants to heal us, and a requirement of healing is to put our weight on Him and accept the covering of His love on our lives, which, incidentally, takes away our fears—fear of the future, financial loss, poor health, loneliness, bad relationships—in fact, fear in all of its forms.

The Woman in 31 is now clothed, and there is order in her life as she receives her self-worth from the Aleph, God the Strength in her life. God gives her value as she leans totally on Him for strength, support, and dignity. He affirms her. He supports her. Then, like the meaning of the letter Samekh, she puts her weight on God as He transfers His strength, love and value to cover her. Now she can laugh and not cry, living life in the best way she can without being afraid of the future.

~

Healing Emotions

The scriptures explain God holds our emotions.

> **"You keep track of all my sorrows. You have collected all my tears in your bottle. You have recorded each one in your book."**
>
> **—Psalm 56:8**

Like the meaning of Ayin, God hears and sees the dark days in our lives, and when we talk to Him in prayer, He definitely answers us. Yeshua gave us the privilege of speaking to God directly and, amongst many things, He said:

> **"Whatever you ask in My name, that will I do, so that the Father may be glorified in the Son. If you ask Me anything in My name, I will do *it*."**
>
> **—John 14:13–14 NASB**

God sees every moment of our days as they play out—every hour, every conversation, every behaviour; He hears every thought. Nothing is missed in our day, even though it may seem that God has missed us. Nothing is missed, and He will answer.

The Hebrew letter Samekh, in ancient times, may have represented a shield; some describe it as a staff. The shield is used for protection, and the staff for support. The Hebrew letter preceding Samekh is Nun, which, as I wrote earlier, means "faithful," "humble," and "life." These letters joined together, Samekh and Nun, suggest someone who is broken but puts their total reliance on God through His Son, Jesus. The two letters are read as the Hebrew word *ness*, which means "miracle." We will understand later as we try to imagine a fragment of the life of a woman in the Bible called Leah.

The Process of Healing

The Bible describes the life of a woman called Leah. According to one perspective of several Jewish writings, Leah's eyes were described as "tender" or "soft" because she constantly cried to God when she prayed. The narrative tells us that, according to family tradition, as the elder daughter, she should be the first to get married. Leah had heard negative reports about the man she was about to marry, so she is described as having "leaned" on God in prayer with tears to express her feelings. God heard Leah's request. She avoided that marriage and was married to someone else. But the story doesn't end there because Leah stepped into a new relationship riding high on emotional pain. It became disturbingly obvious that, although her husband Jacob cared for her, his passion was for Leah's younger sister, Rachel, who became his second wife.

Historic Jewish writings record that having more than one wife was permitted. Although in this case, Leah and Rachel were sisters, they had different mothers, as their father had more than one wife. Although the culture during those times allowed men to marry more than one woman, God's original design was for marriage between one man and one woman. Centuries later, when asked about marriage, Yeshua reminded the people that from the beginning, marriage was between one man and one woman, and this was to continue.

Laban gave Rachel to Jacob after fulfilling Leah's bridal week, but he had to work another seven years for Rachel, the woman he had loved from the beginning. Leah's emotions were probably similar to the pain of an extra-marital affair as we imagine the draining, soul-destroying attempts of trying to redirect her husband's attention. Leah may have watched him daily, using every opportunity to attract his attention, hoping maybe that he would take notice of the smallest detail that somehow would ignite his feelings for her. She would have longed for him to say he loved her the way she imagined he did with her sister. But no, Rachel had won his attention. So Leah redirected her emotional stress to God in prayer.

Researchers have compared the pain of rejection to having hot coffee spilt on your body.[1] Leah would have experienced this type of searing pain with perhaps the low self-image and the many dark feelings that followed, but she continued to pray. As described earlier, the Hebrew letter Samekh, in ancient times, may have represented a shield; some describe it as staff. The shield is used for protection, and the staff for support, as in Psalms 23, where the writer states that God's rod and staff—symbolic of His words of strength and direction—bring comfort. Leah was a broken woman who put her total reliance on God.

---

1. Hannah Rose, "Facing Rejection," Psychology Today, accessed June 2019, https://www.psychologytoday.com/intl/blog/working-through-shame/201906/facing-rejection.

Leah's Eyes

An examination of the adjective "tender," used to describe Leah's eyes, shows it was an ancient idiom to express the idea of a gentle, loving, and caring person. This description gives a deeper understanding of Leah's character, revealing a woman who was gentle, loving, and caring. By describing her eyes, the scriptures aim to draw our attention to the beauty of Leah's character. It is not suggesting that there was something wrong with her eyes, as is often expressed, or that she was less beautiful than her sister.

Time passed, God answered her prayers, and she went on to have six children. Leah's fourth son was called Judah, which means "praise." In the book of Matthew, Judah is listed in the lineage of Yeshua, Jesus. So, we can see that Leah's wait wasn't in vain. She remained consistent and patient in prayer and, like the Woman in 31, I'm sure she "laughed at the days to come!"

The First Stage: Healing Humiliation

Humiliation is a raw and degrading emotion that God recognised in Leah as the first negative emotion, the catalyst for her healing process to begin. Imagine humiliation as an enormous block of stone we place in the way of healing to protect and defend the pain we've carried for years. It causes us to hide from ourselves, from God, and from each other.

Humiliation featured regularly in Leah's life. Every day, she felt powerless as she watched her husband and her own sister, his wife, sharing moments together as her invisible body passed by them, powerless to change his feelings. As time passed, God began a deep work of healing. As mentioned earlier, the scriptures make clear God knew what was happening in the

211

marriage by explaining, "[God] saw that Leah was unloved" (Genesis 29:31). Leaning on God for support to address this crushing feeling was crucial for Leah.

The healing process was gradual. Her first son Ruben signalled that God was beginning to heal this specific area of her life when she remarked, "It's because God has seen how humiliated I have been" (Genesis 29:32 CJB). This was a strong, binding emotion that Leah appeared to live with for some time. Humiliation can crush at the very core, causing low self-image and feelings of worthlessness. Striving for the attention of a man left Leah feeling crushed. So she turned to God for "strength" and to restore her "dignity" over a process of time. And like the Woman in 31, she could again "laugh at the days to come."

The Second Stage: Recognising God Is Aware of the Pain and Learning to Let Go

Emotional wounds are deep, making it hard to unravel where the pain is hitting. There are knots in our lives, and once untied, those threads lead to other dark areas of ourselves or to the instigators of our pain. But God's light is in us.

Leah may have carried the pain of her husband's rejection from their first night together when he realised she wasn't the woman he had been promised after a seven-year contractual agreement. Throughout the next seven years of working for Rachel, his mind would have been on her, trying to get her attention when possible during the day and maybe thinking about her while sleeping with Leah. These are the conclusions we could draw. However, God saw Leah's turmoil, and although He seemed silent, He heard Leah's thoughts and saw her emotions.

"When you go through deep waters, I will be with you. When you go through rivers of difficulty, you will not drown. When you walk through the fire of oppression, you will not be burned up; the flames will not consume you."

—Isaiah 43:2

This second stage of healing is to believe that God hears prayers even though He seems silent. This is called faith or trust. It's an essential prerequisite for the healing process to begin. The book of Hebrews says this: "But without faith it is impossible to please Him, for [whoever] comes to God must believe that He is, and that He is a rewarder of those who diligently seek Him." (Hebrews 11:6 NKJV).

The healing continues, but there is still much inward looking. It's hard to stop the pain of years crammed with memories from the past and the people who hurt us. It's easy to become comfortable with the familiar because we know what to expect; we respond in the same way every time, so we don't need to think. It's as though we become the passive responders to a slow, destructive event in our lives.

Although Leah was still hoping for a better relationship with her husband, I would imagine she was getting a better understanding of the way God was working in her life as she, like the meaning of Samekh, waited on God for support. When we wait, we are still. Our minds are still, and we hear. As a sign that He had heard, God continued to bless Leah by giving her a second child, who she called Simon, meaning "hearing." While we wait, God works.

Emotional healing takes time. I imagine if God healed all our emotions at once, we wouldn't survive the process physically. If you take the biblical perspective that we are first a spirit person, with emotions, a mind and a will, all housed in a body, then healing to the whole person must take place. This is recognised in the Proverbs, which make connections with the whole person:

"Hope deferred makes the heart sick."

—Proverbs 13:12

"A joyful heart is medicine, but a crushed spirit destroys the bones."

—Proverbs 17:22 ESV

"A tranquil heart is life to the body, but envy rots the bones."

—Proverbs 14:30 TLV

As we read the short narrative of Leah's experience, we realise that it was difficult for her to let go of the intense feelings she had. Jacob was her husband, and even though he may not have loved her the way he loved Rachel, he still cared for her and his children.

It can be hard to let go. My "letting go" process happened over a period of eight years, on and off. It shouldn't have taken that amount of time, but as I wrote earlier, I buried the pain and tried to move on. It didn't work because, like Leah, Father needed to heal my emotions in the same way. But at the end of the eight years, when I decided to let go, I experienced a new beginning.

Leah names her third child Levi, meaning "joining," in what I would describe as a last attempt to win her husband's love. We have to admire Leah; she desperately wanted to be joined to her husband, but Father wanted her to let go of the pain. We also need to let go of the pain.

The Third Stage: Learning to Trust and Praise

This is the crucial stage when Leah begins to trust in the strength of God's character and His ability to heal all her wounded emotions and, like the Woman in 31, replace the damage with "strength" and "dignity." She's no longer focused on her husband (or situation) in the same way but realises her energy was better placed on God, her Strong and Powerful Leader who loves unconditionally. It's at this stage we accept no one can heal but God; no one can heal the past and all its pain but God, and no one can guarantee the future but God. So, we thank Him and trust His process.

At a later stage in her life, Leah's trust has increased, and Judah, her fourth son, is born. Thanks to God's healing in her life, Leah's confidence is growing, and she calls her son "Judah," meaning "Praise!" There is evidence of a process of healing that is gradual but complete. The writings in Psalm 145, verse 14, read: "The Lord helps the fallen and lifts up those bent beneath their loads." Now Leah, like the Woman in 31, wears the "clothes" of "strength" and "dignity." Her emotions have healed, and as she lifts her head, she—like you—can laugh at the days to come!

Chapter 16

The Power of Words

PEY
When she opens her mouth, she speaks wisely;
on her tongue is loving instruction.

Two young women, my middle sister Georgia and me, aged seventeen and twenty, decided it was time to experience something new. We would often lie in bed in the room shared with our younger sister, Leah, talking and laughing late into the night and sometimes early morning. Our thoughts and conversations raced over futures filled with hope, optimism, excitement, and innocence. We loved listening to music and singing. Georgia loved to dance, so with this motivation we joined a choir which we hoped would introduce us to new experiences, new people, and new friends, as well as give us the chance to sing.

This joining together of voices across London and the surrounding counties was the first initiative of its time and attracted young people across the UK. We got through the audition and were immediately "joined" to a large group of women. These were exciting times, and our week was filled with rehearsals and busy weekends singing in different venues, from schools to concert halls and recording and TV studios. Rehearsals ended late into the evening, and when we weren't able to get a lift home, my sister and I found ourselves standing at the bus stop, waiting for the late bus home. Summer was kind, but winter always tested our commitment to sing.

We were young, with little experience with life and different characters. As far as we were concerned, the common interest that brought everyone together was sufficient to develop some sort of trust. Our belief was soon dismantled as we realised not everyone shared the same view, and for whatever reason, we were misunderstood amongst a small group of women. We had joined the choir with a few male friends our age with whom we had grown up. We discovered social events were being held outside of rehearsals and soon realised our friends had become part of the group that kept us out. Still, we were determined to commit even though the close bonds we developed growing up as friends were beginning to unravel as we drifted apart.

Despite age, women can find themselves the target of jealousy, a strong emotion that feels uncomfortable for me to even write about. And when we misunderstand each other, if not recognised and addressed, it can be dangerous, hurtful, and devastating in subtle ways.

One afternoon during a time of group reflection before a performance, we were asked to hold hands as part of a joint focus. I happened to be standing next to a woman who, for whatever reason, could no longer hide her feelings. On that day, at that moment, her emotions exploded, and she refused to link hands for the well-rehearsed, pre-performance joint gesture of unity. It hurt. My sister and I carried on, again choosing to ignore the noise, overlook the offence, and sing! Years later, Father reminded me of that time and my need to forgive so He could heal the memory of that day and time and heal me.

Georgia and I eventually left the group as our lives took turns that would begin a long separation, but not before we finally formed friendships amongst a few women in the group that lasted well into our later adult years. Looking back, I realised that rather than women taking time to get to know each other, words rocked with suspicion and jealousy caused missed opportunities for friendships. Like the Woman in 31, God wants to fill our mouths with words to encourage and build.

As Women, we have the power to support each other into our destinies if we can move aside insecurities and fears when we perceive others with qualities we would like to have. Knowingly or otherwise, when we use our thoughts and words to dismantle other women's lives, we invariably build or dismantle our own. But when we use our words to build, the effect is strength. Let's ask God to show us ourselves so we can heal, support, and bless each other. Women need each other for strength.

The Mirrors

It was a sweltering summer afternoon as I queued for the changing rooms in Zara, a high-street women's clothing shop. I re-counted the hangers to make sure I wasn't carrying more than the number allowed in the fitting rooms. The wait was long, and the large industrial metal fan whirred furiously to keep shoppers and staff cool, yet made little impact as the hot air simply redistributed. Everyone was hot.

The large, floor-to-ceiling mirrors seemed to have been carefully positioned on the wall where we waited. I'm not sure whether this was to give an optical illusion of bigger floor space or for women to glance at their images. Whatever the reason, I don't think the mirror helped, as every couple of minutes, other women and I glanced furtively only to quickly turn away. We either did not want to appear as if we cared or felt unsatisfied with the woman looking back. For those more confident, a gesture was given to push back the hair from their face or look approvingly at the image. I thought I had reached a stage of having a balanced view of my body image until the woman who looked back at me appeared older, with tired eyes. *I should have put on more makeup*, I remember thinking, or maybe I needed a needle intervention! Maybe. I quickly looked away, remembering that I was beginning to accept the woman God had called and created me to be at this stage of my journey.

Standing at the front of the line, I was relieved when the sales consultant finally counted the number of clothes and quickly handed over a large number tag for the fitting rooms. Feeling hot, the worst moment to try on clothes, I stepped inside the cubicle, hung the items, and began to undress. As I rolled the dress down over my "temporarily tightened for a flat appearance stomach," I heard a long, laboured sigh from the adjoining room, followed by the remark to the assistant who she had asked for advice.

"The dress is lovely," she said with a sigh, "but I'm not!"

The woman in the adjoining changing room wasn't at all bothered about who heard because that was simply how she felt.

~

The Meaning of Pey

There isn't enough time to fully explore and discuss the strength and importance of this Hebrew letter and the linked twenty-sixth verse, but what we understand is this: words are *powerful*. In the right context, they boost confidence, encourage, and motivate; on the other hand, they can destroy. As it says in Proverbs 18, verse 21:

"The tongue can bring death or life; those who love to talk will reap the consequences."

At some point, we have been the recipient of cruel words as part of gossip stemming from jealousy, fear, offence, or insecurity. And, if we're honest, we also have misused words.

Words are so powerful that the writer of this prayer said this:

"Take control of what I say, O Lord, and guard my lips."

—Psalm 141:3

The letter *Pey*, pronounced "pay," has the number value eighty and is the seventeenth letter of the Hebrew alphabet. The number seventeen is a mixture of the Hebrew letters Yod (10) and Zayin (7) and represents victory and completeness. Similarly, the meaning of the number seventeen mirrors the number value eighty for the letter Pey, meaning "strength." The symbol for the letter Pey looks like a mouth, symbolising words, speech, or expression.

The Hebrew letter Ayin appears before Pey, and as described earlier, Ayin means "eye" or "understanding." It suggests that a person must understand before being able to speak. The writings of Proverbs chapter 18, verse 13, say that to answer someone before hearing him out is both stupid and embarrassing. Yes, I'll be the first to hold my hand up to that!

God speaks, His words are powerful, and scripture tells us Jesus is the Word made flesh:

> **"Christ became a human being and lived among us. We saw His shining greatness. This greatness was given to Jesus from His Father, He was full of unfailing love and faithfulness."**
>
> **—John 1:14**

The opening scriptures of the Bible begin with God speaking His thoughts into tangible realities. For us, it's an ongoing process of listening, recognising what He is doing in our lives, and getting on with what we need to do by putting our words into action.

Our culture is visual. We're constantly bombarded with photoshopped, altered images from social media, drawing us into a perception of beauty to fit cultural aspirations. And despite whatever age we may be, this idealised world can blur the boundaries of reality. The images are not always true representations, yet we are drawn in from either the perspective of a consumer or a supplier of our own lifestyles to others. Life-size images on outdoor advertising, the display of celebrity lives on social media, or the momentary snapshots from the lives of others all feed more information into our internal narrative of how we should present ourselves, with a continuing assault on our confidence. But what and who are the real mirrors? With many strong, carefully constructed images dictating or suggesting how women should look, it's sometimes hard to turn away from the crafted suggestions; even if we remain unaffected, they prove difficult to ignore. For the woman in the fitting room, the mirror reflected the image of the woman she held in her head.

Having had time to build confidence and self-esteem over the years, I'm now at the stage in my life where I'm better able to give compliments without expecting anything in return. I'm still learning how to receive compliments without the feeling of appearing self-absorbed. However, that doesn't reduce how often I still glance in the mirror or want to change an aspect of my appearance; I'm not there yet—I'm working on it. I'd like to think I'm working on myself for myself and not for the daily media injections of acceptability. Most importantly, and set apart from my attempts, Father is working on me.

Compliments

I came across an article in *Psychology Today* titled "Why Women Can't Accept Compliments: The science behind why females seem to put themselves down,"[1] posted on March 29, 2016, by author Jen Kim. In it, Kim refers to an Amy Schumer YouTube video[2] that briefly examined women's reactions to compliments. Kim writes,

Amy encounters a typical group of attractive young women

---

1. Jen Kim, "Why Women Can't Accept Compliments," Psychology Today, 2016, https://www.psychologytoday.com/intl/blog/valley-girl-brain/201603/why-women-cant-accept-compliments.
2. Amy Schumer, YouTube, May 15, 2013, https://www.youtube.com/watch?v=hzlvDV3mpZw.

who all greet each other with big smiles and generous compliments: "Your hair is amazing." "I love your hat." Instead of gratitude, the complimented women respond with sighs and hilariously self-deprecating retorts: "I tried to look like Kate Hudson but ended up looking like a Golden Retriever's dingleberry." "Are you drunk...? I look like an Armenian man. People are trying to buy carpets from me."

Kim continues,

It's satire at its best—slightly exaggerated but its sentiment, still painfully true. When one of the women actually accepts a compliment with a gracious "thank you"—a foreign concept to the group—they all turn on each other in a murderous rampage. In real life, the homicidal killing spree would likely be replaced with silent judgement and incredulity. *"Did she really acknowledge how great she is? She is so conceited!"*

A compliment is defined by the Oxford dictionary as "a remark that expresses approval, admiration, or respect." Knowing this is a regularly debated topic, and opening up the discussion is similar to treading murky water, I tentatively ask this question: why can't we truly compliment each other—not flatter, but compliment—without expecting anything in return? Is it something to do with fluctuating levels of self-esteem rooted in the strong emotion called jealousy, described using the simile, "as cruel as the grave" (Ecclesiastes 8:6 NKJV)?

> **"Do nothing out of rivalry or vanity; but, in humility, regard each other as better than yourselves—look out for each other's interests and not just for your own."**
>
> **—Philippians 2:3–4 CJB**

If we can't verbally compliment, then find other ways to encourage and support. Depending on our communication strengths and needs, an inability to do this suggests a need to uncover our own issues, and that's okay. We need to look to God, the Aleph and Strong, Powerful Leader of our lives, the One from whom we get our confidence and self-image, as He works to build us up to a level where we can truly appreciate the best in other women.

~

Pey

Pey is about the delivery of words—spoken, whispered, and proclaimed—from one mouth. The Woman in 31 speaks wisely when she opens her mouth. We can use our words to change lives as we carefully release each word to each other. Over time, and experiences preferably forgotten, we learn to think before we speak. Before opening our mouths, we can ask God to give us the words to say. Words become active when we give words a voice; until then, they remain thoughts.

The words of the Woman in 31 are described as "loving instruction." Of course, we generally won't hear an audible voice, but God speaks to our spirits through nature, friends, people we trust, dreams, and the scriptures—in many ways.

I recall one dull January winter afternoon when I was thinking deeply about a few unresolved issues. As my husband drove along the dreary street with its assortment of houses and corner shops interspersed with large dark factory buildings, we came to a stop at the traffic lights. I glanced over towards the small petrol station on my left, and tucked away on a wall in the corner was an advert that read, "Please believe these days will pass." I couldn't believe what I was reading and laughed out loud as I pointed Andrew to the sign.

Father was reading our thoughts and chose to answer in an advert. It wasn't by chance because that year became the catalyst for many significant changes on an accelerated scale. God had spoken. There are so many opportunities for God to speak; we just need to look and not restrict Him to the ways we know. Be open and expect Him to speak, knowing His Words will always confirm the written Word.

Chapter 17

Staying Focused

TSADE
She watches how things go in her house,
not eating the bread of idleness.

Watching My Mother

From a child, I was always preoccupied with doing something. As the eldest, if it wasn't helping my parents care for my siblings, it was making elaborate two-storey houses from cardboard boxes fitted with tiny beds, chairs, and tables carefully cut out, glued, and painted. There was always a plan for the day and, later, a plan for my life; being idle wasn't a concept I understood.

With five young children, four within a year apart of their birthdays and two years between my younger brother and me, my mother was busy, so there had to be a plan for her family, and there was no time for being idle. I recall the mornings we would walk through the back streets, lined with rows of tiny, terraced houses leading to the train station. Mum kept a brisk and steady pace, and I'd often find my little legs running alongside, trying to keep up in compliance with her gentle but firm instruction, "Stretch your legs!"

During my childhood and into my twenties, my mother worked a full-time career in the criminal justice system to support her family. During the winter months, snow, rain, grey days, and on to the gratification of summer months, she tirelessly worked a five-day week, from nine to five, to give her family the best start she could. The first year of my study beyond school was spent in a college quite near her work. At lunchtime, I would often jump on a bus to take the short journey to her workplace. There, in the canteen, I would be rewarded with a large lunch and a stodgy currant sponge with custard for dessert.

Mum had a great rapport with her colleagues and was liked by all. God made her days great and gave her success at the work in which she prided herself. Not one to sit around, her weekends were filled with serving her local church where we grew up. And now, reflecting on that time, I don't know where she got the energy, but like the Woman in 31, I believe it came from the enthusiasm for her activities and God's strength, as she relied on Him.

Later, as adults, Dad often brought up the topic of Mum's love and loyalty. Mum, of course, would remain modestly silent. It was during those conversations we learnt from Dad that, in the early days when we were very young with a small income and "five mouths to feed," Mum would often go hungry to make sure we had enough to eat. There was no time for Mum to sit around waiting for life to happen—no time to watch lives on social media; her time was spent "watching the affairs of her household" and "not eating the bread of idleness." That was the work ethic in which I grew up.

~

The Meaning of Tsade

Tsade is the eighteenth letter of the Hebrew alphabet with a numerical representation of ninety. In Hebrew, eighteen is the number of life, and the number ninety signifies life to its fullest. Sarah, the biblical matriarch mentioned in an earlier chapter, embodied the essence of Tsade, giving birth to her only son, Isaac, at age ninety.

Tsade is linked to the twenty-seventh verse, and the letter formation has the connotation of a man lying down. Taking a deeper look into the meaning of the word, it symbolises a person who is humble, who realises they are in need and looking to God the Father for support as they trust Him. This letter also represents "a righteous person," but there is no righteousness, or you could say, "right standing" outside of Yeshua. When we look to God through His Son, Yeshua, He lifts us up and gives the strength to succeed in life.

> **"Therefore, humble yourselves under the mighty hand of God, so that at the right time he may lift you up. Throw all your anxieties upon him because he cares about you."**
> **—Peter 5:6–7 CJB**

The Woman's "house" referred to in the verse is symbolic of her life as she, like us, looks to God for support in the direction her life is taking. Although time can be spent admiring aspects of people's lives through social media or other forms, there is the danger of not being happy with our own lives. Maybe it's a natural human curiosity, interest or fascination with the lives of others, but our ideas, self-conceptualisation, and beliefs are subtly being shaped, changed, challenged, or reinforced by the observations we make and our continual interaction with the culture in which we live. Let's engage with our image and "like" our own lives.

I spent a lot of time observing my life, watching how things were playing out and trying to fit the puzzle pieces into my inset. That, of course, had some merit, yet praying and listening but not acting correctly regularly caused trouble, and some of the decisions I made were costly. It's natural to act with hindsight, but Father doesn't mention hindsight. He speaks of "vision," which redirects our attention from looking backward to forward while listening and making the right decision. One well-known verse in the book of Philippians says, "But one thing I do: Forgetting what is behind and straining toward what is ahead..." (Philippians 3:13 NIV).

God says:

"'For I know the plans I have for you,' declares the Lord, 'plans to prosper you and not to harm you, plans to give you hope and a future.'"

—Jeremiah 29:11 NIV

We make plans, pray and get on with the business of life, knowing that God will make the right connections for us as we work. Like the Woman in 31, this is the way we "watch how things go" in our lives.

Chapter 18

Productivity and Accomplishment

QOF
Her children arise; they make her happy;
her husband, too, as he praises her.

When I left 131, the first and last home I owned with my first husband, I recall standing in the doorway of the main bedroom gazing towards the room opposite; for that brief moment, it felt as though time had stopped. Time had stopped for me to reflect and move to a new phase of my life. The memories we shared came racing back like flicking through pictures on a mobile, and at that moment, I sensed it would be a long time before I would ever own another home.

God at Work

Many years passed, and deep down I kept to the belief that God was going to give me my own home. No more moving. After marrying Andrew, although we had spoken many times about buying a home, lost in the day-to-day routines, I was beginning to feel like the vision was fading. I would listen to women talking about their home renovations, extensions, and furniture—discussions of permanence—and deep down, after fourteen moves, I longed for my own home. Having met and married mid-way in our lives, Andrew and I needed time to build finances, and living in the UK—especially London—had priced many out of the property market.

To fuel our vision to own property, we would often drive into wealthy neighbourhoods and return home motivated. On one particular day, I lost hope and began to have serious doubts about ever owning a home. I stopped wanting to drive to beautiful neighbourhoods to look at property and talk about where we might choose to live; doubt silently turned to bitterness, and the dream of owning a home faded.

The Meaning of Qof

Qof is the nineteenth letter of the Hebrew alphabet and is connected to the letter Tsade. Qof represents holiness, which is the state of being set apart for God through His Son, Jesus the Christ, who is our Holiness before God. The Hebrew word for "set apart" is *kadosh*, and Qof is the first letter of kadosh.

Theoretically, holiness embodies the idea of moral and ethical purity as lived, modelled, and taught by Yeshua, who is righteous and gives us right standing before the Father. The living experience, however, can be likened to gazing into a mirror and seeing our image reflected back. Using this analogy, as we look into the mirror, we see God looking back at us. We are reflecting His image in perfection—His holiness.

David, in the writing of Psalms 51, verse 10 (ESV), makes the request, "Create in me a clean heart, [O] God, and renew a right spirit within me." The life, death, and resurrection of Yeshua give us the ability to be holy before God through the help of His Holy Spirit working in our daily lives.

Children and Honesty

Because the Woman in 31 has found her identity in God, she experiences success and productivity as she trusts Him. The word "children" in the verse can be symbolic of productivity and accomplishment. Her "children" represent the good things she has produced in her life, and they affirm her. Like the Woman in 31, we are able to rely completely on God for everything we need on a daily basis. And when we go down on our knees in honesty about where we are struggling, in honesty of our needs and feelings even though we may be angry with God, and in honesty of the way we feel, we can be sure that He hears us and will answer.

Many years earlier, Father had clearly spoken in a dream where I saw myself walking down a street not far from a large, open green space. I heard Him say, "Go in trust." In the scene I knew I was going to buy property. My negative emotions escalated that week and peaked while watching a programme one evening where people were discussing homes. My emotions crashed as my husband silently looked on from a distance and wisely said nothing. Experiencing a complete meltdown, I walked into the bedroom, lay on the bed and cried for a long while. I was angry with God. I couldn't understand why I had to wait so long and seemed no closer to owning a home. Fourteen moves on, I was simply tired.

That night, God spoke to me in a dream about separating the productive from the unproductive areas in my life. I later realised this was part of the process of healing my emotions as I described earlier in the book. When I woke, it felt as though I'd spent several sessions with a counsellor, and over the weeks that followed, although I cried at times, I realised that Father was healing me.

So, who are the Woman's "children" said to rise and make her happy? As well as the literal meaning, they refer to the plans, visions, and hopes that God will fulfil as we trust. It's true that not all the ideas we plan are realised, but eventually we will see the best of what we have asked for. Despite the many suggestions, there isn't an answer for the time it takes to see the dreams we have hoped and worked for. However, the process of seeing things realised isn't an unfulfilled cycle because, while we wait, our characters are being developed, and we are learning from experiences. As important as realising the dream, the journey is about evolving into the Woman God has created us to be. Then, by the time opportunities arrive, we're stable, ready, and equipped.

Chapter 19

The Future is Now

RESH
**Many women have done wonderful things,
but you surpass them all!**

The Meaning of Resh

This is a declaration of greatness! It is God telling women they have excelled, accelerated, and achieved amazingly. *Resh* is the twentieth letter of the Hebrew alphabet and is the number in the Bible that deals with expectancy, the ability to make life applications to what has been learned (wisdom), leadership, and waiting for great things to happen. The number twenty in the Bible is linked to silver, and this precious metal symbolises the act of redemption: God's Son, Yeshua, exchanging His life for ours to give us a new beginning. Resh is linked to the number ten, represented by the Hebrew letter Yod, which speaks of power and God's right hand of strength and deliverance (power to pull us out of trouble). Psalm chapter 89, verse 13 says:

"Powerful is your arm! Strong is your hand! Your right hand is lifted high in glorious strength."

The ancient symbol of the letter Resh is linked to the twenty-ninth verse. It resembles a person's head and is interpreted as a head bowed to God, the King of Glory, who stooped low to serve us. The Creator of all things lived among us in a human body, yet is fully God. Amazing! Hosea, in chapter 11, verse 4, talks about God's loving care, describing God bending down to feed the people He loved. In addition to the literal meaning, we can apply those Words to our lives.

The opening words in Genesis, the first book in the Bible, begin with the Hebrew word *Bereshit* (pronounced "beresheet"), meaning "in the beginning" or "source." This opening word directs the reader to the Head of the House, God, whose Son is Jesus. Resh is connected to the Head, and the Head is connected to Wisdom. The Woman has turned to God for knowledge, experience, and good judgement for making the right decisions; she is far-reaching and productive.

∼

Appreciation Through Her Hair

There are many women in the New Testament—the second part of the Bible—who turned to Yeshua for understanding and healing in their lives. A classic story, one of many, is of a woman called Mary Magdalene who connected to Jesus using the beauty of her hair. It seems very much like Resh in action as Mary bowed her head to the King, the ultimate act of wisdom. Using the most expensive perfume of her time, she washed and oiled his feet with her hair.

I believe Mary was gifted with beautiful hair to bless Yeshua, the Son of God. My Dad used to ask, "What's in your hands?" Whatever God has given us, whether we choose to call it a gift, talent, or ability, we should give it back to Him by serving others. This is the ultimate, highest act of service and Resh at work in our lives. Furthermore, this is how we prosper. We may not recognise it at first, but as we allow Father to heal our lives, we will uncover abilities that were always there but unseen.

Mary Magdalene's oil and hair were precious. She demonstrated an action beyond words, which describes the passion and quality of the work women are capable of when we "bow our heads"—giving our lives to Christ and opening our minds and hearts to the King. This act of completely opening up or abandoning herself to God gave Mary complete healing, and she was grateful beyond words.

Connecting to the Woman

The path women have forged through the centuries and the incredible successes they have achieved, and are still achieving in countless areas, has been phenomenal. History is full of pioneers in culture, finance, science, medicine, business, the arts, missions, politics, sport, literature, and so much more. Turning the spotlight on ourselves in connection with the Woman in 31, we see that her ability to achieve in all areas stems from her identity, and as I have mentioned, identity comes from God. In multiple ways, He continues to work in our lives and our character development as we choose to accept Father as the Resh, the source of strength and powerful leadership, and trust Him to work in our lives.

The detailed discussion of the Hebrew letters is given to add a layer of meaning, depth of understanding and connection to the

Woman's character and skills, with each letter directing us to Christ. Of course, I want to emphasise that our lives are not dictated by numbers or letters but led by Christ. The meanings of each Hebrew letter simply paint a rich tapestry of colour and shapes, allowing us to see Christ in us and the work He is doing in our lives.

By studying the Woman in 31, we get a clearer perspective of who we are, where we are going, and how we will get to the destination. The development of these characteristics is *a lifetime* process. We will be regular visitors to the various stages at different times in our lives, but each visit will strengthen our character. Remember, it's not a linear journey of character development but cyclical steps, where each characteristic seen in the Woman is developed through her life experiences. The process starts in our hearts, hearts that turn to the Great God, the Source, who created the woman to be like Himself.

"So God created human beings in his own image. In the image of God he created them; male and female he created them."

—Genesis 1:27

Achievements in our daily lives may not reach the centre stage of world recognition, but those such as raising our children, relationships with our husbands, parental or caregiver relationships, and family and friends form the foundation of a healthy society. Whether we play a role in education, politics, sports, the church, military service, the financial world, arts, innovation, run our own business, or work for the public or private sector, we will always impact the lives of people we meet through the gifts, talents, abilities and passions and, crucially, the words we say backed with actions.

People Watching

As mentioned earlier, it's simply human nature to people-watch, either positively or negatively, but when we do what I describe as "life by life" comparisons, it becomes a downward spiral as the boundaries and rules will keep changing. It's easy to do, and if we're honest, we can get caught up. Stop comparing yourself to others and stop trying to live up to the expectations of others. Review how you spend your time. Father is the Head and Source of your life, the Aleph, and He is bending down to lift you up so you can accomplish your plans. God has given every woman a vision, passion, interest, desire to accomplish, skill, and talent, and He has given you everything you need to be successful.

Womb Time

At the very beginning of life, Creator God commanded the man and woman to be fruitful and multiply. This instruction hasn't changed and is reinforced when we make the declaration: "I AM Fruitful!" Remember, this statement is not based on what is happening in your life right now. Thinking about a woman's womb and the darkness that fills it, something amazing is being created behind closed doors. On closer inspection, it will not look like the finished product. I've named that time in life "Womb Time." It's not supposed to be seen by your family, friends, or work colleagues because it's about what God is doing in your life during the "hidden years." I spoke about this earlier when we explored Mem, but I wanted to reinforce the point.

Routines

There's power in life's routine. This is what Father taught me, and I live by that precious statement. Daily routines bring consistency, stability, reliability, the understanding of processes, realising how you function, opportunities to better manage time, relationships, health, and money; it's an endless list. The Bible describes a day in the life of Rachel, who met her husband on her regular route to work, and the rest is history. As a result of staying consistent in her everyday routines, she became an exemplary woman who would be the subject of discussion well into the future.

Imagine

Imagine if we could meet ourselves at each important stage of our lives. What would we say to our woman? Would we turn away with negative feelings or congratulate her? Would we comment positively on her hair, weight, clothes, or achievements? Or would we say she made the wrong choices, needed to lose weight and change her image, hair, makeup, and clothes, or should be older or younger—an endless list of negatives? Would we look away in shame, unable to forgive her past? Or would we show acceptance, realising she did the best with what she had, appraise her strengths, and recognise the work in her life is ongoing?

Earlier, I described the woman in the changing room, who looked at the woman in the mirror, staring back and saying, "The dress is lovely, but I'm not!" When we aim negative words at ourselves, we rarely miss. If I weren't turning words on my hair, I'd use them to express dissatisfaction with my weight;

I aimed negative words at my professional career and fed the constant drive to bring my work to painful levels of perfection. I regularly presented these standards to the woman I looked at in the mirror, then judged her when things didn't march according to plan. The woman looking back at you needs you to appreciate and love her for who she is. By stepping into humanity through His Son Jesus, God bent down to love *you*. Look again, make the necessary revisions, and stop aiming negative words at yourself.

The Future Is Now

Consider this statement from the verse: "Many women have done wonderful things." What does that statement mean? On the one hand, it acknowledges achievements women have made, and on the other, it is saying *your* success in *your* life can't be compared to those of other women. Father has already seen you as having "surpassed them all" in the life and work He has given *you*. And as the scriptures tell us, God has already seen the end result:

> **"Only I can tell you the future before it even happens. Everything I plan will come to pass, for I do whatever I wish."**
>
> **—Isaiah 46:10**

When we sleep, we all dream. We may remember the details or not at all. If you are interested in this area, begin by asking God to help you recall your dreams. When we dream, sometimes God shows us snippets of future events in our lives, and from the moment we "see" the event, it has already happened. We only need to see it played out as our lives match up at the right time, and God makes the dream a reality. So, yes, many women have indeed done wonderful things, but you *and* the woman in the mirror have outdone them all!

Chapter 20

Seeing Beyond Beauty

SHIN
Charm can lie, beauty can vanish, but a woman who fears Adonai (The Lord) should be praised.

Beauty has been debated for centuries, and as we explore the meaning of the letter *Shin*, we'll see that beauty can be used as a tool to build or destroy. From one perspective, it can be used to the woman's advantage. That was the case in the story of Queen Esther, who was able to save a nation from annihilation by using her beauty, amongst other character qualities God had developed during her time of preparation. The queen used her beauty, prayer, and fasting as a tools to argue on behalf of a nation, and she won. On the flip side, a woman called Delilah used her charm and beauty in a deceptive way to find the strengths and weaknesses of her man, with the intent of killing him; she cut down his strength progressively.

With societal and cultural perceptions of beauty used to accept or reject images, beauty at a base level can be used as a tool to divide women through comparison and competition. Without positive female role models for advice and support in times of emotional vulnerability, we have the propensity to turn on ourselves, which amongst other behaviours, can manifest as negative self-image, low self-esteem, and even self-loathing.

The Meaning of Shin

The twenty-first Hebrew letter, linked to the thirtieth verse letter, is three multiples of seven and the number for perfection. Among other interpretations, it can mean "an appointed time," and its number value of three-hundred means "God appears." Early visual representations of the number looked like flames of fire and can be interpreted as teeth. Additionally, while fire consumes in a destructive manner, teeth consume food to build the body. One destroys, and the other nourishes.

Fire can also be interpreted as a passion. In the book of Deuteronomy, God is described as a "consuming fire" who passionately went ahead of the life journey His people had to make. He did this to show them where to go and to protect them from the dangers ahead. Today, He remains at the forefront of our lives, working with us in the same way.

Shaping

Our concept of beauty is shaped early in childhood. As young girls we look to our mothers for love, a sense of self, affirmation, and approval. If fathers are present in our lives and able to encourage us on that level, we hold onto their words and love. Beyond parents and caregivers, women such as grandmothers, aunts, family friends, and significant others play important roles in our lives.

Fathers

Fathers, grandfathers, and trusted male family members are critical in shaping and raising daughters and developing self-esteem. It wasn't always the words my father said but the gentle and loving way he raised me that helped shape me into the Woman I am today. His actions, such as the hands-on role he played alongside my mother in our home to support his large family and the wise advice he gave me while I was growing up, were also important.

My Dad had a way of gesturing with a "nod of approval" when my sisters and I experimented with hairstyles and clothes. He would sometimes remind me of how much I looked like his youngest sister, who was known for her looks and love of fast cars and lived on the Caribbean Island of Dominica, where he grew up. He gave many affirmations, and I needed them all to form the woman I was to become.

Presenting a positive role model of male behaviour and observing how he was with my mother at home was just as crucial to a little girl growing up into a young woman—his loving and gentle ways, the debate and subsequent laughter that would occasionally burst through their hushed voices.

Mothers

As part of developing identity, I believe mothers are more "hands on" in the daily nurturing and shaping of their daughters. My mother was, and still is, beautiful to look at, with her petite frame and a never-diminishing sense of style. The early years of gruelling hard work bringing up five small children from babies to young adults unravelled as experiences she would later share with other young mothers. She had the job of shaping the development of three girls into women. It was my mother and aunt who played a part in influencing my identity at that early stage, allowing me to find my emerging self. As sisters we experimented with clothes, colour, makeup, and hairstyles inspired by the glossy images of *Vogue* and the monthly *Ebony* magazines, featuring pictures of women of colour and endless ideas on hairstyles and cosmetics.

I was around six years old when my mother took me to London's Oxford Street. She held my hand tightly as we walked along the wide pavement crammed with shoppers and tourists. Looking up, people appeared like giants with their long strides, and the many shops and department stores we passed looked imposing as they lined the street to attract potential customers. The picture of my first coat remains a vivid image. My mother bought me a beautiful emerald-green, double-breasted wool coat with large brass buttons, complete with a belt and a metal buckle. I wore the coat as soon as she purchased it. I remember the bright green colour, the smell of new fabric and the feel of the new wool coat. I felt very special. Moments in the shaping of our identity become landmarks. These are the times that help to chisel out the women we have become. They become fixed points in our memories.

My mother leaned her head towards me and gave my hand a gentle squeeze.

"What do you want to be when you grow up?"

The question stirred destiny inside of me. I was wrapped in the vivid emerald-green, double-breasted new wool coat, complete with brass buttons and a large belt.

"Mummy, I want to be..."

I'll leave my response unsaid for now, but let's just say it was the defining of the identify of a little girl with big dreams and an even bigger vision!

Beauty with Lines and Wrinkles

It's been said that civilisation and every philosophical system have sought the meaning of beauty. On one level, it's about the pursuit of youth glamorised by the cosmetic industry. Shopping for makeup before I got married to Andrew, I found myself wandering through the maze of beauty counters in a large London department store. The bright lights and colour palette of the advertising displays, the powerful aromas, with a mixture of music and voices hung in the air. Unsure of where I wanted to stop, I continued to stroll past a line of sales consultants armed with bottles and stretched arms ready to spray the latest aroma onto willing customers.

I finally stopped to buy foundation, and during the conversation with the sales consultant, without mention of my age, the subject turned to the need to buy a serum to combat the first lines and wrinkles. I remember looking at my smooth face thinking, *really?* I couldn't see any wrinkles or fine lines in the areas I thought to be important, so I didn't see the point.

And even if I had, wouldn't the wrinkles and fine lines presented on my face have shown a woman emerging on her journey?

As I walked back through the noise and excitement, I realized the experiences I had developed over time had given me enough to understand the woman I wanted to present and how I wanted to present her. Now I was the one in control, and I made a choice. I walked away with just the foundation wrapped in the shiny yellow bag with the famous logo.

In life events, experiences shape and build our character. In this sense, I define "character" as an inner beauty shaped where no one can see. This is the real beauty. It isn't subject to the superficial brush strokes of societal norms, and its hidden ability is powerful enough to attract the attention of the people we meet, leaving lasting impressions. Beauty comes out of our mouths, leads our actions, shapes our attitudes and supports other women in the process of their becoming.

The beauty of the Woman in 31 is tied to God's perfection. This is possible because of His continual presence in her life, strengthening her character and pushing her forward. Externals play a part, but it's acknowledged that God's life lasts when the beauty fades.

Chapter 21

Knowing Your Identity

TAV
Give her a share of what she produces;
let her work speak her praises at the city gates.

"It was on a night like this that I found myself in a repeating pattern of running and walking in the heavy rain along the long, dark side road leading to my home. I was filled with anguish and remorse, and clashing thoughts moved around my head with kinetic energy. My life was an emotional mess; I had made an idiot of myself again, and I felt weak and foolish."

During the writing of this book, I dreamed I was running on a dirt road. It was a narrow, long road with no room for anyone else. As I ran, I could hear the sound of my breathing as you do during a run. However, I realised I wasn't running alone as there was someone running in the distance. I sensed it was important to keep the person in view. Without going into too much detail, as I ran, there were many obstacles I had to overcome, one of which was a gate that looked like a wide and high wall made from concrete. I realised the only way to get past was to speak to the gate using the command "Open!" And as I spoke, the concrete gate moved aside but only slightly, so I pushed it aside and continued to run, keeping who I call the "pacemaker" in sight.

I didn't fully understand the dream at the time, although its symbolism seemed relatively "easy" to interpret. But I have learned to wait on God's Spirit to understand, as things do not always mean what they seem. I now realise the "pacemaker" in the dream is God, known to us through His Spirit and given to us by Christ Jesus.

Having seen this dream, my motivational phrase became, "Push with both hands!" Although situations in our lives may sometimes present as "brick walls," they are not walls but "gates" that can be pushed aside. There is always *hope*. Recognising that what we see as a wall is indeed a gate, empowers us with a solution: we need to push. Then there are times when we are honoured to have others push with us, and we push together. We need each other. I encourage you to never take a person's help for granted. Agree with the many words in the writings that tell us it is God who sends people into our lives to help. He will always send others to help; God has made us complete and will not leave us lacking.

The Meaning of Tav

The Hebrew letter *Tav*, pronounced "Tarv," with a number representation of four-hundred, is the final letter of the alphabet. As we have seen throughout, if we choose to look below the surface of each letter, we understand that each

Hebrew letter is significant in its meaning and can help us understand our life journey and faith in God, through His Son, Jesus Christ. In its earliest written form, Tav was shaped like a cross from which the interpretation of "mark," "sign," "seal," or "covenant" was derived.

In the last book of the Bible, God announces Himself as the *Alpha*, the first letter of the Greek alphabet, and the *Omega*, which we know as the last letter of the Greek alphabet. In Greek, "Alpha" means "first" or "most significant occurrence," and "Omega" means "great" or "the end of all things."

"I am Alpha and Omega, the beginning and the ending, saith the Lord, which is, and which was, and which is to come, the Almighty."

—Revelation 1:8 KJV

The Hebrew word for Alpha is called Aleph (the first letter of the Hebrew alphabet), and as I have described throughout, it means "head," "strength," and "leader." The Hebrew word for Omega is Tav, (the last letter of the Hebrew alphabet) meaning "mark" or "sign." The early representation of Tav looked like two sticks crossed.

Jesus declared, "I AM the Beginning and the End," "I AM the Alpha and Omega," or "I AM the Aleph and Tav. An interpretation could read: "I AM the Head and the Sign or Mark," or "I AM the end or fulfilment." During the time after Jesus' resurrection, Thomas, one of His followers, stood in disbelief until Yeshua showed the mark of the crucifixion nails in His hands. Only then did Thomas believe. When we put our lives and trust in Jesus, He places His mark or seal on us, and Father gives His Spirit for guidance, strength, healthy minds, and so much more to help us live our everyday lives. As we put our trust in Yeshua's accomplishment for us, God helps us be productive in everything we do "be(ing) fruitful in every good work," as described in Colossians 1, verse 10.

~

The Journey of the Woman

In the book of Genesis, the Complete Jewish Bible makes references to the man as "man-person" or *ish* (in Hebrew) and referred to as "Adam" in English translations. The name of the first "woman-person," as described in the CJB, is actually called "woman" or *ishah* (in Hebrew). In English, she is known as "Eve."

The woman-person—Eve (ishah)—was taken out of Adam, the man-person (ish).

> **"And Adam said, 'This is now bone of my bones, and flesh of my flesh: she shall be called Woman, because she was taken out of Man.'"**
>
> **—Genesis 2:23 KJV**

Later, as Ishah makes what I call her "woman journeys," and a further understanding of her name unfolds to *Havah*, sometimes spelled *Chava(h)*, meaning "life," she becomes the "mother of all life" (see Genesis 3:20 LEB) or "mother of all natural life." This is not the same as God's Life (*Chayim*) since *Havah* became the Mother of all people on Earth.

From the moment we hold our children, whether we have given birth or adopted, unless other events occur, we experience the joy and amazement unique to having produced a tiny human being. After the pain of giving birth comes joy, which in every way supports the Bible statement: "Weeping may last through the night, but joy comes with the morning." (Psalms 30:5). We were created to be productive in every area of our lives. Despite the obstacles, pain, darkness, loneliness, unkind words, and so much more, women were created to produce.

My father described God's DNA as "design nature attributes," which are His building blocks in our lives as women. His design nature attributes (DNA) give us the ability to produce, in fulfilment of God's first instruction to "be fruitful and multiply." And Yeshua's completed assignment gave us the ability to continue in this way.

> **"Then the way you live will always honour and please the Lord, and your lives will produce every kind of good fruit. All the while, you will grow as you learn to know God better and better."**
>
> **—Colossians 1:10**

God promises that as we follow His advice, whatever we put our minds to will be successful.

> **"[I AM] like a tree planted by streams—[I] bear fruit in season, [My] leaves never wither, everything [I do] succeeds."**
>
> **—Psalms 1:3 CJB (personalized)**

I have personalized this by inserting "I" and "my." You can do the same.

From the Beginning

From the beginning of time, Father's heart for the Woman was to be productive in everything. In Genesis, the first book of the Bible, the twenty-sixth verse (CJB) of the first chapter reads, "Then God said, 'Let us make humankind in our own image, in the likeness of ourselves; and let them rule over the fish in the sea, the birds in the air....'" Then later, in verse 28, it says, "God blessed them: God said to them, 'Be fruitful, multiply, fill the earth and subdue it....'" Women alongside men were created to be producers.

God first referred to men and women as "humankind," as translated in the CJB. "Then God said, 'Let us make humankind in our image, in the likeness of ourselves....'" Then in the next clause, God says, "and let them rule over...." It is clear that God had the woman in mind, and she was given authority from the moment God spoke His Words.

Later in verse 28, God blesses both the man and the woman, saying, "Be fruitful," and later uses the words "multiply," "fill," "subdue," and "rule." God gave the man and the woman authority. God creates the animals, and the man names them. But despite having seen all the animals in God's creation, the man could not find another "kind" that looked like himself. So, God put the man into a deep sleep, and He revealed a side of his glory through ish (man), and then isha (woman) became the completion of Adam's unveiling. Genesis 2, verse 21 (JUB), says, "and He took one of his sides (ribs), and He closed the flesh in its place." The next verse reads, "And the Lord God built the side that He had taken from man into a woman, and He brought her to man." Isha came from Ish's side, equal yet different but blessed.

The Woman Stands Alongside, Equal Yet Different but Blessed

It is said (in Genesis 2:22) the woman was made from the man's "rib," which is consistent with the majority of English translations of the Hebrew manuscript. The Hebrew word for rib, *tsela*, could be translated as "chamber," "plank," "side," and even "compartment."

The discussion about whether Isha was made from a rib is called the "rib theory." Opposing arguments from some Jewish leaders explain the Woman was made from Adam's side and even other areas of his body.[1] Whichever view we take, what we do know is that God took some physical part of DNA from Adam and formed Eve. I've briefly mentioned these areas because it's important to understand that God created the woman *alongside* the man; she is not inferior in any way. He drew her out of Ish (Adam) with the ability to produce, and that is my point. It's good to debate and discuss as we sharpen each other, as long as we don't come away from the founding principles of Yeshua's work; we receive this free gift through trust.

There are or have been times in our lives, however, when we haven't felt productive at all. In fact, it felt like we stagnated, came to a stop, unsure of how to move forward. We made seemingly failed attempts to make ideas successful, tried to build our lives, and more could be said. At our lowest, we may even have felt useless, having hit a brick wall. But God, from

---

1. Biblical Archaeology Society Staff, "The Adam and Eve Story: Eve Came From Where?," Biblical Archaeology Society, November 26, 2024. https://www.biblicalarchaeology.org/daily/biblical-topics/bible-interpretation/the-adam-and-eve-story-eve-came-from-where/.

the beginning of time, blessed us with everything we needed to build and move forward.

During the course of writing this book, it became increasingly evident that the theme throughout the entire description of the Woman in 31 was *identity*. For years, she has remained a mystery, an ancient poetic description of perfection, an allegory, a symbol, a subject of teaching and discussion amongst women, yet remaining ever more hidden. Identity is the centre of who we are as individuals, and it strongly influences thoughts, behaviours, and decisions. It is the dividing line between the confident woman and the insecure woman. It indicates and measures our level of success or delay on a daily basis and affects long-term plans. I purposely used the word "delay" rather than "failure" because I don't believe we fail, but we can "delay" plans that have the potential to be realised sooner.

It took years to finally understand that my success was wrapped up in understanding who I was—*my identity*. Was I my father? Did I have the strength of my mother? Did I have the confidence of the women I met at various stages in my life? Did my background fit? Would my contribution to the discussion be accepted? Would others think I didn't have enough knowledge? Would my home be accepted? And what about my financial status? It was an endless list, a continuous assault of negative questioning until Father began to show me my identity through *His* character qualities. He used my life experiences to develop His character qualities, which I later understood could be seen as "spiritual emotions." The Bible talks about love, joy, and peace, described as "the fruit of the Spirit." Analysed further, these qualities are what we could describe as "emotions" because we literally feel these responses. How then does this work practically?

I have discovered that when I feel the negative and long-term toxic emotion of anxiety, I literally ask Father for His peace for that moment. I may then search for words in the Bible to address those feelings. I then speak them out loud, over and over, to meditate and cause His Words to take effect in my day. This spiritual emotion then begins to erase the negative human emotion, and I begin to settle. Over time, peace, or *shalom* in Hebrew, meaning "wholeness," "completeness," or "perfection" in all areas of our lives, increases to become a deep-seated part of character through God's strength. "For I can do everything through Christ who gives me strength." (Philippians 4:13). Then I become the Woman in 31.

I am learning to respect the processes in my life, even though they have not always followed my timeline targets for achievement or completion, and this has required a further quality of patience, an emotion, skill, and character quality that God gives. Now, this time, I am running my life with purpose and direction, with a better understanding of my road while recognising God's leadership and others who help me push aside the obstacles.

Identity Brings Strength

The Woman in 31 is secure in who she is—her identity—and this strength has allowed her to be successful. We could correctly assume that she is no longer comparing herself to other women. Her journey requires different types of character strengths at different stages to respond to the demands of her home, workplace, family, and relationships. Yet, despite all this, the Woman in 31 is still able to orient in a tough and demanding world. She is able to do so because she understands the centre of who she is, her core identity, and her strength in

God, who remains the consistent, Strong and Powerful Leader in her life. God is the centre, and because of this, she can "laugh at the days to come."

So, who is this perfect Woman in the perfect world of Proverbs 31? She is the character qualities of Jesus Christ being formed in us, just as the amazing statement from Galatians 4, verse 19, assures, "until Christ is formed in you." The Woman in 31 is every woman, in *every way*, at every stage of our lives, irrespective of how we see ourselves. Whether the vision is realised or incomplete, starting out or midway, we are the Woman in 31 who is emerging every day we look in the mirror. We are this Woman on Monday morning whether we feel disengaged and switched off or wide awake and ready to take the challenge. We are her when we laugh or feel crushed in pain. We are her when we are full and when we are empty. This Woman is God's greatness and His character qualities working through our lives.

We are the Woman in 31, united in diversity of culture, economic background, age, and physical features. United, yet diverse, but united by the Woman in 31 because *she is* all of who God is, perfect in every way, united with us through His Son Jesus, Yeshua.

Omnipresence and omniscience are God's attributes, yet He lives in us and in His fullness. We are drawing on God's character qualities to live. I will explain.

In John 14 (ESV), Jesus said: "If anyone loves me, he will keep my word, and my father will love him, and we will come to him **and make our abode in him**." This tells us that the fulness of Christ (who IS God) lives in us.

Colossians 2:19 (NKJV) says, "For in Him dwells all the fullness of the Godhead bodily, and you are complete in Him."

Every day we are drawing on the fullness of who God our Father **is**. The scriptures in Matthew 5:48 (KJV) make the statement, "Be ye perfect as [I am] perfect." We are drawing on the perfection of God's character in us to reflect Him in all that we do.

Based on John 3:5–6 (NIV), we are born of the Spirit. Jesus said to Nicodemus, "Flesh gives birth to flesh, but the Spirit gives birth to spirit" in us who are born again. God gives birth to spirit from His Spirit. We are like our Father.

This is a journey of unfolding and discovering who you are In Christ Jesus. God said to Abraham, "Walk before me and be perfect." Enjoy the journey one step at a time.

Life will give us a share of the good things, and we will produce. We will be appreciated and honoured for what we do. I've often heard people say, "The best is yet to come," and have silently asked, *When?* Now I realise, many experiences later, my "when" starts now. Our "best" starts today. With help from other women, as it arrives, and with God at the centre, we will continue to "push" at life "with both hands."

AM I?

Young enough?

Pretty enough?

Slim enough?

Old enough?

Healthy enough?

Wealthy enough?

Educated enough?

Articulate enough?

Tall enough?

Dressed enough?

Motherly enough?

Caring enough?

Interesting enough?

Liked enough?

AM I enough?

ENOUGH!

I AM ENOUGH.

I AM the Woman in 31.

Bibliography

Biblical Archaeology Society Staff. "The Adam and Eve Story: Eve Came From Where?" Biblical Archaeology Society, November 26, 2024. https://www.biblicalarchaeology.org/daily/biblical-topics/bible-interpretation/the-adam-and-eve-story-eve-came-from-where/.

Fletcher, Elizabeth. "Clothes in the Ancient Land of the Bible." Women in the Bible, October 25, 2022. http://www.womenintheBible.net/Bible-archaeology/clothes_ancient_Bible/.

Jay, Meg. *The Defining Decade: Why your twenties matter—and how to make the most of them now.* Twelve, 2013.

Kim, Jen. "Why Women Can't Accept Compliments." Psychology Today, 2016. https://www.psychologytoday.com/intl/blog/valley-girl-brain/201603/why-women-cant-accept-compliments.

Rose, Hannah. "Facing Rejection." Psychology Today. Accessed June 2019. https://www.psychologytoday.com/intl/blog/working-through-shame/201906/facing-rejection.

Schumer, Amy. YouTube, May 15, 2013. https://www.youtube.com/watch?v=hzlvDV3mpZw.

The *Miseducation of Lauryn Hill*. Vinyl recording. Ruffhouse: Columbia, 1998.

Acknowledgments

To my sister, Georgia – your constant support and encouragement helped propel this book from a mere idea to the publisher's hands. I am endlessly grateful for your belief in me.

To my husband, Andrew – thank you for the years of deep conversations, for your insights that sparked new perspectives, and for your patience as I poured my heart into these pages.

To my publisher, Winners Press – your timely encouragement and those well-placed emojis brought much-needed lightness to the editing process. Thank you for being my cheerleader and for believing in the message of this book.

About the Author

Brenda Heron is a consultant speech and language therapist with more than twenty-three years of experience working with neurodivergent children, adults, and their families to foster effective communication. As a wife, mother, and former assistant pastor, she served for over fifteen years in her late father's ministry in London, where she mentored, counseled, and taught countless women. Driven by a desire to bridge the ancient and the modern, Brenda spent years studying and teaching the Proverbs 31 woman, helping women connect timeless wisdom to their everyday lives. Her father's passing led to a pivotal seven-year journey to demystify this biblical figure, shaping her passion for empowering women to walk confidently in their purpose. Brenda is also a United Kingdom patent holder with a keen interest in design and innovation.

Connect with Brenda

3onewoman.com

instagram.com/3onewoman

www.ingramcontent.com/pod-product-compliance
Lightning Source LLC
Chambersburg PA
CBHW070548130626
46556CB00001B/69